A Child's First Library of Learning

Things Around Us

TIME-LIFE BOOKS • ALEXANDRIA, VIRGINIA

Contents

How Is Chocolate Made? 4
How Is Bread Made? 6
Why Doesn't Food in Cans Spoil? 8
Why Does a Hard-Boiled Egg Spin Faster Than a Raw Egg? 10
How Does Rice Grow? 12
Why Does Swiss Cheese Have Holes? 14
How Do So Many Fish Get to Market? 16
How Are Cups and Plates Made? 18
Where Do We Get Electricity? 20
How Does a Thermos Work? 22
Why Does Water Put Out a Fire? 24
Why Do Burning Things Make Smoke? 26
Why Won't Oil and Water Mix? 28
Where Does Gasoline Come From? 30
What Happens to Trash? 32
How Does a Telephone Work? 34
How Does a TV Work? 36
How Does a Piano Make Music? 38
How Does a Record Make Sounds? 40
How Are Pencils Made? 42
How Does an Air Conditioner Cool a Room? 44

hy Does a Fan Make a Breeze? 46
hy Can't We See Clearly Through Frosted Glass? 48
hy Do We Stir Bath Water? 50
hy Do Bathroom Windows Steam Up? 52
hy Does Soap Take Dirt Out So Easily? 54
w Does a Washing Machine Clean Clothes? 56
w Do Erasers Remove Writing? 58
hy Does Rubber Stretch and Then Shrink? 60
hy Does Steel Rust? 62
hy Do Magnets Attract Steel? 64
w Does a Magnifying Glass Work? 66
hy Does Soap Make Bubbles? 68
w Does Glue Work? 70
hat Happens to Letters That We Mail? 72
w Does a Vending Machine Work? 74
hy Can't a Car Stop Quickly? 76
hat Do We Have Here? 78
You Know What These Things Are? 80

owing-Up Album 81

How Is Chocolate Made?

ANSWER Chocolate is smooth and creamy. But it's really made from beans! Cacao beans are roasted, then made into a powder. This is mixed with milk, sugar and flavoring to make the candy.

How it grows

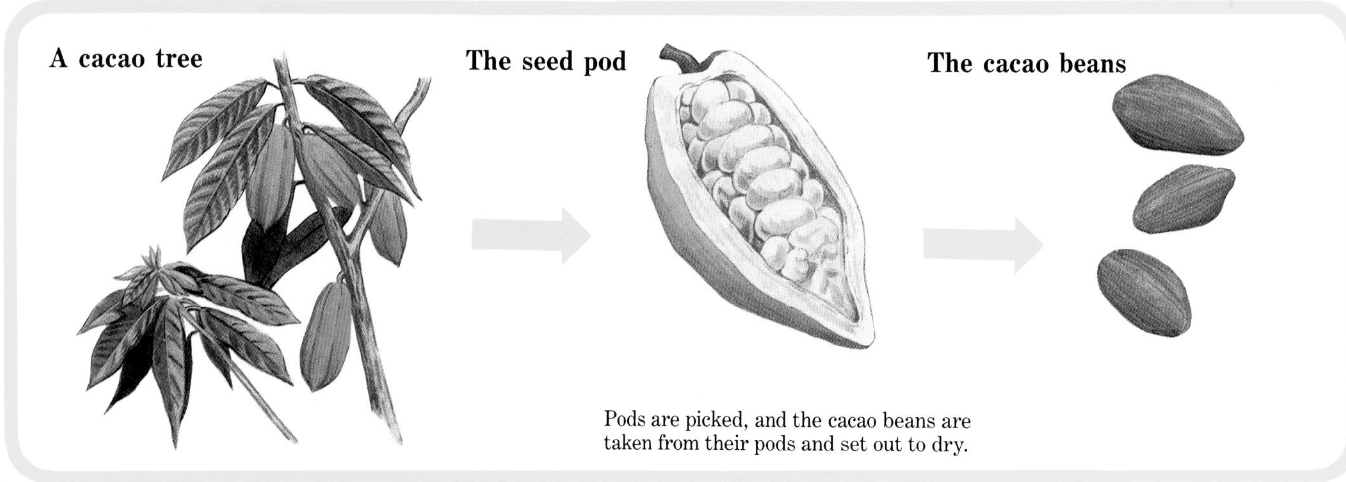

Pods are picked, and the cacao beans are taken from their pods and set out to dry.

Cacao Becomes Chocolates

▲ First all the beans are washed very carefully.

▲ After that big machines grind them into a powder.

▲ Mixing in milk, sugar and flavors makes it creamy.

▲ The chocolate mix is poured into molds and left to harden.

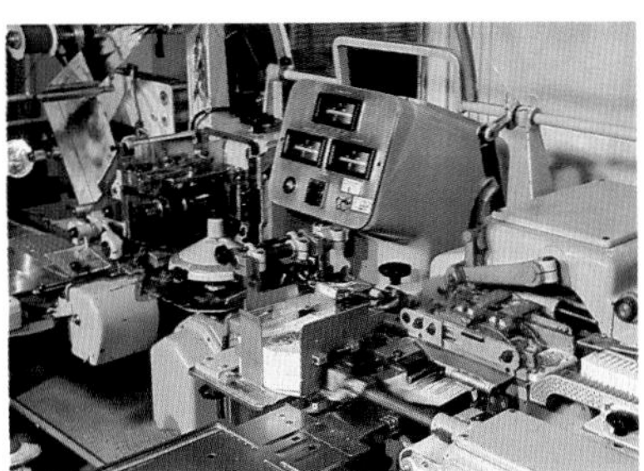

▲ Last the wrapper is put on. Now it's a chocolate bar!

Made from cacao

Cocoa powder, suntan lotion and face creams are some of the things we use that are made from cacao beans.

MINI-DATA

Long ago people living in Mexico and Central America used cacao beans as money. Hernán Cortés, who conquered the Aztecs, was once served a drink made from cacao in the court of the Aztec ruler. He introduced the drink to Spain, but it was almost 100 years before it spread to France in the 17th century. After that chocolate spread rapidly throughout all of Europe.

● To the Parent

Cacao plants grow in the tropics. The countries of the Ivory Coast, Ghana and Brazil are the world's largest producers of cacao beans. Natives of Mexico made the first chocolate, and it was introduced to Europe in about the year 1500. The first known chocolate bar was made by the Swiss in 1876 and became popular throughout Europe. The cocoa powder from which hot and cold cocoa drinks are made is also a popular cacao bean product. Cacao in various forms has been a long-time favorite.

How Is Bread Made?

Bread comes from the oven, of course. But before it is baked, many things must be done. Wheat flour is mixed with water and yeast to make dough. The yeast makes the dough stay soft as it bakes.

You can make bread in your kitchen. Once the dough is ready, cut it into shapes like animals, stars, trees or whatever you like. Then bake them and eat them!

How to make bread

▲ Mix flour, water and yeast. The dough has to be squeezed and turned over and over.

▲ Pat the dough into loaf shapes, and leave them to rise a bit.

Look! It's getting bigger!

▲ Put them in the oven to bake. Soon you'll have fresh bread!

Mmm, let's eat some right now!

Bakeries Make Thousands of Loaves a Day

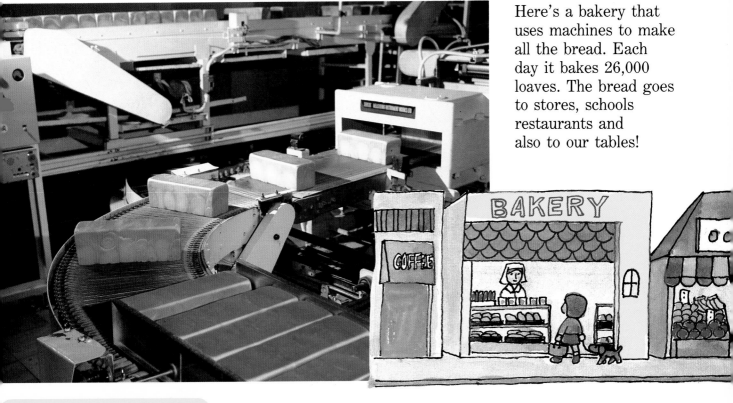

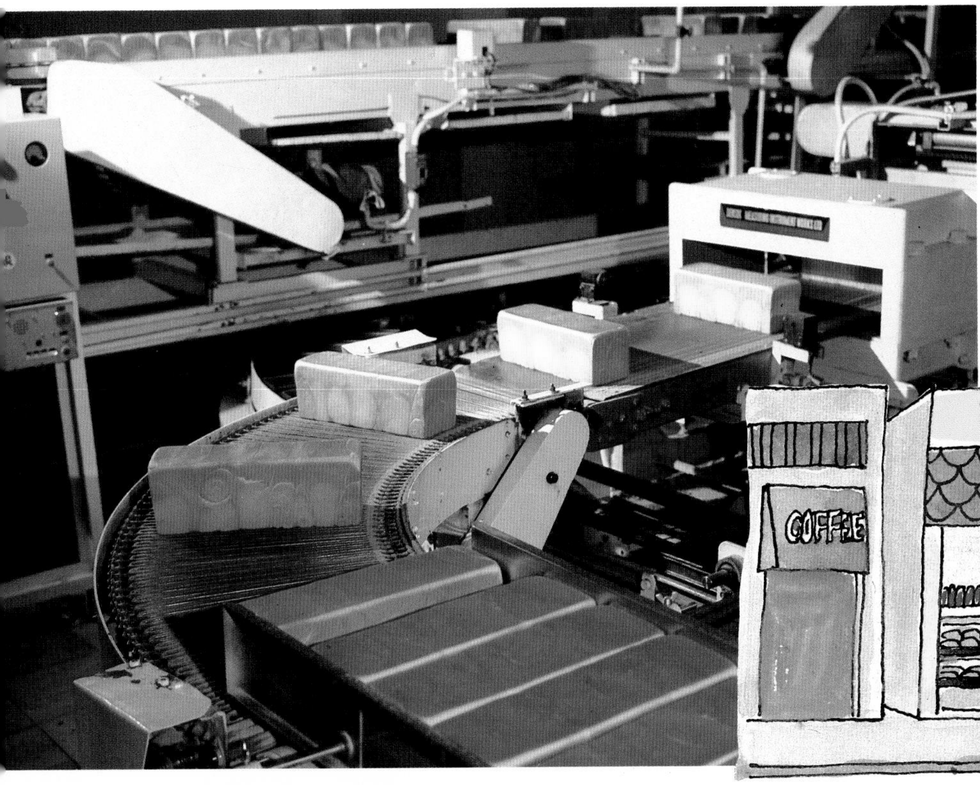

Here's a bakery that uses machines to make all the bread. Each day it bakes 26,000 loaves. The bread goes to stores, schools restaurants and also to our tables!

Bakery products

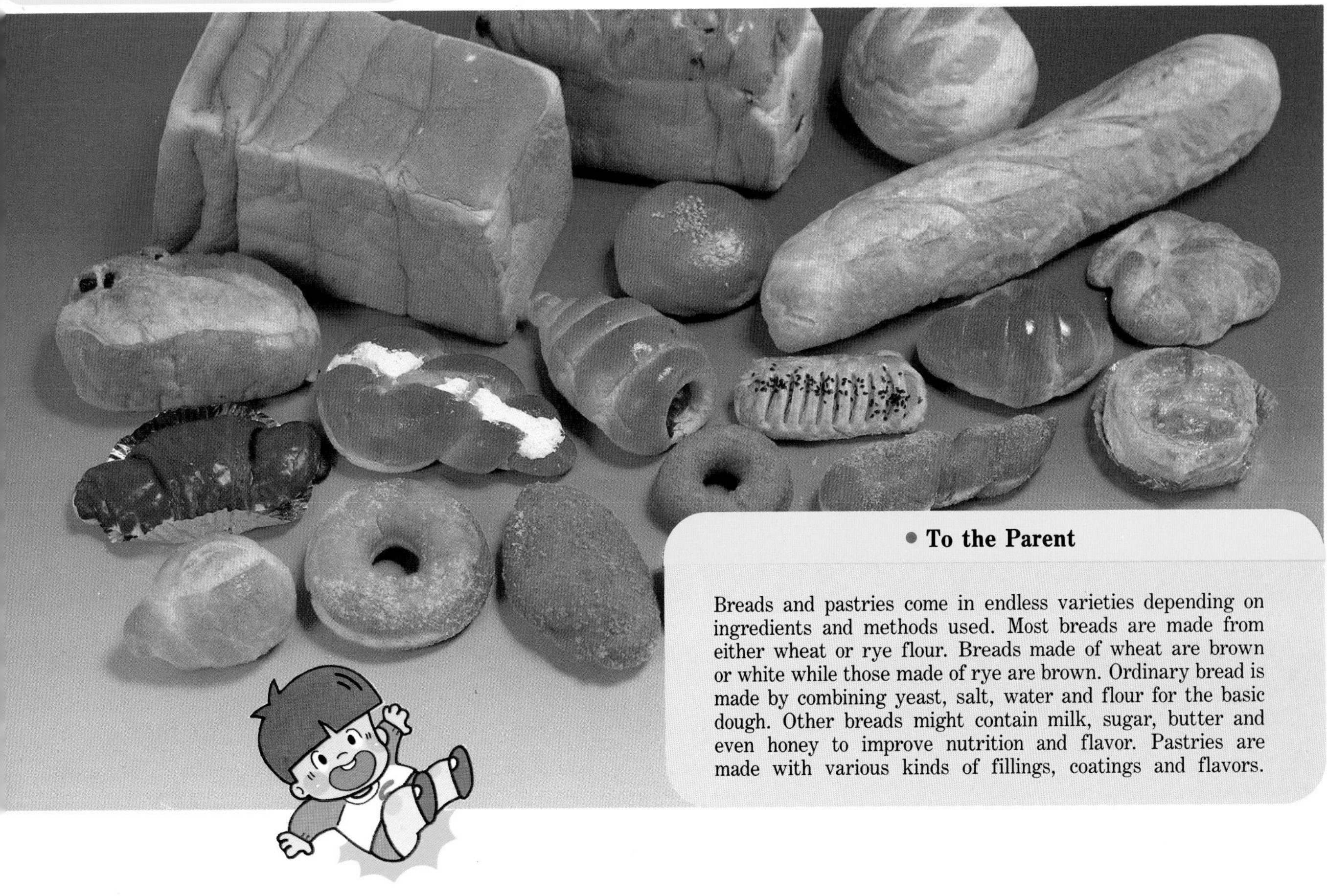

• To the Parent

Breads and pastries come in endless varieties depending on ingredients and methods used. Most breads are made from either wheat or rye flour. Breads made of wheat are brown or white while those made of rye are brown. Ordinary bread is made by combining yeast, salt, water and flour for the basic dough. Other breads might contain milk, sugar, butter and even honey to improve nutrition and flavor. Pastries are made with various kinds of fillings, coatings and flavors.

Why Doesn't Food in Cans Spoil?

Food spoils when it's left out too long. Germs get into it, and that's what spoils the food. Germs are in the air all around us. Cans seal out air, so germs can't reach the food.

We're germs, heh heh! We make all sorts of food go bad — to spoil your dinner!

Oh, oh! It's sealed — we can't find a way to get inside anywhere!

How fruit is canne

First the fruit is cleaned, then juice or syrup is put in the can with it.

Some More Ways to Keep Things From Spoiling

Vhat's the most important thing to do o make sure nothing spoils? See that erms can't live around the food.

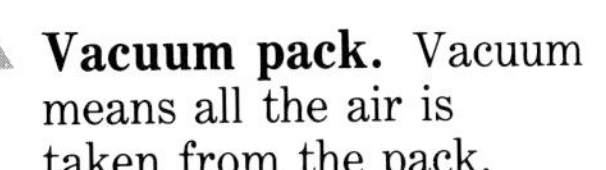

▲ **Vacuum pack.** Vacuum means all the air is taken from the pack.

▲ **Dried foods.** Water is taken out, so germs can't eat.

▲ **Refrigerator.** It's just too cold for germs to get moving.

▲ **Salting.** Lots of salt can also kill all the germs.

Special containers

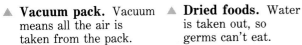

Some foods and drinks come in special kinds of containers. They're made of cardboard, glass, plastic and other things. Some are heated just like cans to kill germs inside.

▲ **Glass**

▲ **Paper**

▲ **Plastic**

The lid is sealed onto the can by a machine.

Then the cans are heated, so the germs inside are all killed.

• To the Parent

Ordinary cans are things that are familiar to every child. They are normally made of steel coated with tin, or all of aluminum. The canning process involves the preparation of the food, filling, removing air from the can, sealing, heating to sterilize, cooling and packing. You might show your child some examples of dried, salted, canned and vacuum-packed foods that you have at home. You might also include some things like freeze-dried, smoked or even frozen foods.

Why Does a Hard-Boiled Egg Spin Faster Than a Raw Egg?

ANSWER If you spin an egg the inside is pulled this way and that. All that moving slows the egg and throws it off balance. A hard-boiled egg's inside is solid, so its parts can't move.

TRY THIS

If you heat an egg enough, it turns hard

Ask your mother or father to heat up a frying pan, and break an egg into it. Watch how it turns hard, step by step.

▲ At first the clear part is very clear.

▲ Then it gets hotter and begins to harden.

▲ When it's really white it's all done.

Where Do Chickens Lay Eggs?

In some countries farmers keep chickens in long buildings. That makes it easy to collect the eggs they lay.

▲ These buildings are the nice clean homes of chickens that lay eggs for people like us.

▲ See how it works inside? The eggs roll down into long trays to be picked up for market.

Eggs make many of our foods

▲ Custard

▲ Layer cake

▲ Sponge cake

▲ Mayonnaise

▲ Ice cream

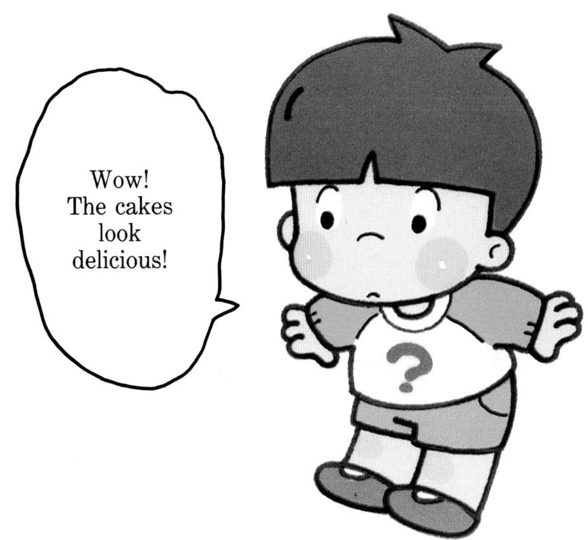
Wow!
The cakes
look
delicious!

● To the Parent

To demonstrate the difference in spins between a boiled egg and a raw egg merely pick a flat surface and set both eggs spinning as you would two tops. Due to the liquidity of the raw egg the spin's force is not completely transmitted to its contents. Instead, they spin a bit more slowly than the shell, reducing overall speed. An egg white turns hard at about 176° F. (80° C.). The yolk, however, needs less heat and will begin to turn hard at a temperature as low as 153° F. (67° C.).

How Does Rice Grow?

Grains of rice are actually the seeds of the rice plant. Rice is really a kind of grass. It usually grows in water, so planting and raising it is very hard work for farmers.

▲ Rice looks like this after it's harvested.

After picking, rice stalks are used for straw.

▲ **Straw**

I am a mat made from dry rice plants cut into straw.

● To the Parent

Rice is recognized as one of the world's great food staples. It is eaten not only by itself as a cooked dish. It is also useful as the base of many other foods, condiments and even of some of the world's most popular beverages: beer and sake. It is used to make foodstuffs, crackers, vinegar, vegetable oil and other familiar items. Wet-rice farming is one of the oldest forms of agriculture known and is the foundation of many great civilizations. Most children will be delighted to learn the whole cycle that brings rice to their tables: planting it into seed beds, transplanting it to the fields, then irrigation, harvesting, threshing, drying and polishing. Every one of these jobs is still done by hand in many places.

The husks on each grain are taken off by a big machine after harvest.

▲ Even the husks are dried and made into fertilizer.

▲ Next the grains are milled. This rubs off all the brown coating, which is bran.

The husks are removed to make brown rice.

▲ The rice is polished and is ready to cook.

In Asia rice is eaten even on picnics in the form of rice balls.

Why Does Swiss Cheese Have Holes?

ANSWER When Swiss cheese is being made, it sits and hardens. A gas forms bubbles in it. When the cheese is finally hard, the bubbles are the holes.

How Cheese Is Made

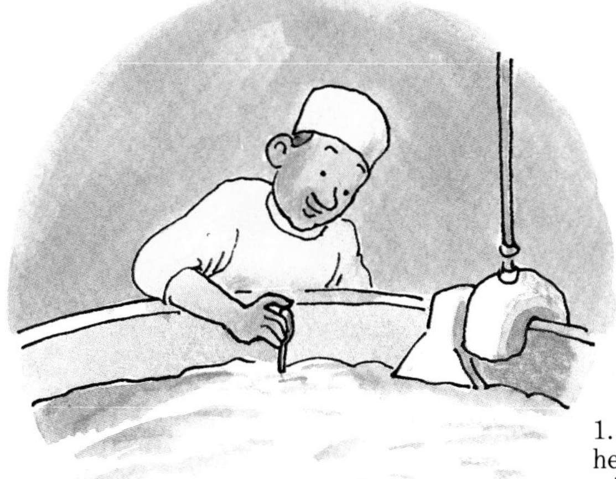

1. Milk is heated and mixed with tiny things called bacteria. That makes the milk turn sour.

2. The sour milk is mixed with natural chemicals and stirred until it is solid.

3. The solid pieces are cut into chunks and then put into molds for shaping.

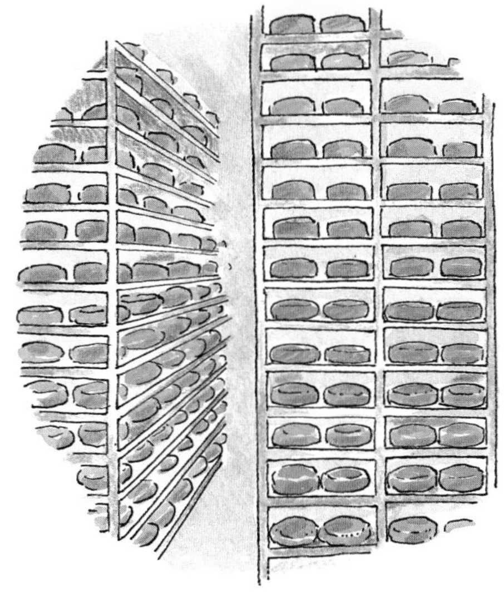

4. The cheeses are removed from the molds and set aside to ripen. That's when they get their flavor.

Some European cheeses

People everywhere eat cheese. What's your favorite kind?

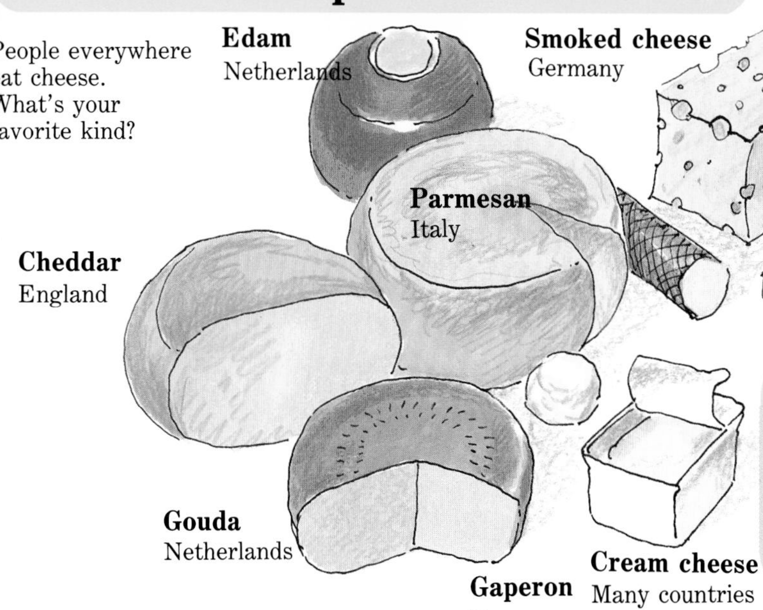

• To the Parent

In the cheesemaking process, bacteria are mixed into milk to sour it. Rennet, a substance with enzymes, is added to curdle the sour milk. Salt is added and the curd is shaped in barrels or molds. It then may take from a few weeks to a year to ripen or age. Carbon dioxide bubbles from bacteria create the holes in Swiss cheese.

How Do So Many Fish Get to Market?

ANSWER We eat fish that come from oceans, lakes, rivers and ponds. Men and women who fish bring their catch to a few big markets every day. At these markets a dealer from your local store buys fish for resale.

▲ **Catching fish at sea**

Fishing boats go out to sea to catch fish to sell. Some of them must go very far, even to other countries. They're gone for months.

◀ **Raising fish offshore**

Some people have found another way to catch fish. They raise them in pens or tanks, just like farm animals.

Not all fish are sold in markets. Some go to factories where they are made into fish cakes and other kinds of food.

At the port

Fishing boats and fish farmers bring their catch first to a special market on a pier where boats are easy to unload.

Trucks take the fish to big markets in the city. They must be moved right away so they won't spoil.

The big markets in the city sort out all the many kinds of fish for people who come from local stores. Your local storekeeper buys the fish there and sells them to you.

• To the Parent

The ocean fishing industry has two sectors: deep-sea and coastal. The deep-sea fishermen fish throughout the oceans of the world for bonito, haddock, herring, shrimp, tuna and other kinds of fish. They sell their catches to brokers at markets in their home ports. The brokers ship the fish to big wholesale centers. Store owners buy their stock there daily to take back home for resale.

How Are Cups and Plates Made?

ANSWER Cups, plates and bowls are made of clay. First clay is mixed with water to make it soft. Then it is molded into the right shape and baked in ovens to make it hard.

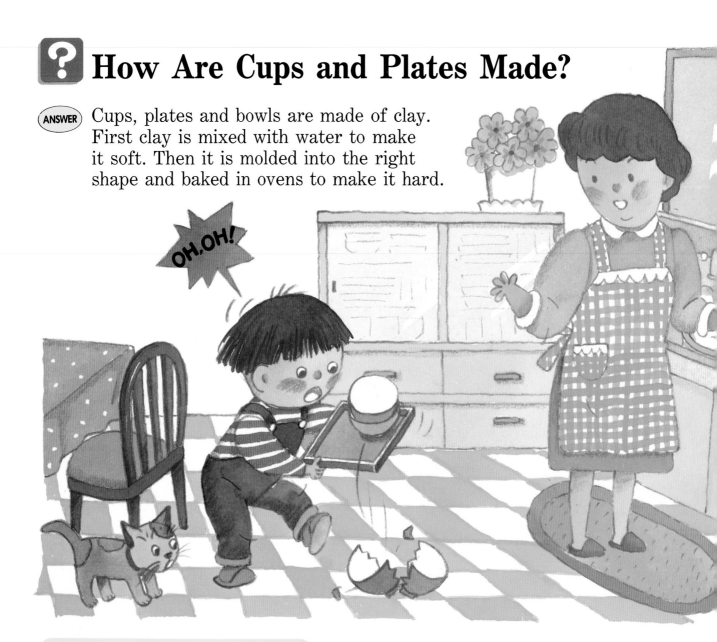

OH,OH!

How pottery is made

▲ A shape is made from clay.

▲ Cups are dried in the sun.

▲ Designs and shiny coats go on.

Other Kinds of Tableware

▲ Glass

▲ Plastic

▲ Wood

▲ Metal

▲ The things are baked in an oven.

● To the Parent

For ceramics that are to be used in the household, a special clay is mixed with substances like mica, feldspar or silica, depending on the use and finish planned. The clay is shaped on a potter's wheel or in a press, then is dried and finally fired in a kiln. This produces an unglazed ware such as that used for plant pots. To finish dinnerware, glaze is applied and the piece refired. Porcelain is thinner and harder than earthenware. It is translucent and rings clearly when struck.

Where Do We Get Electricity?

ANSWER Electricity seems to come from holes in the wall, doesn't it? Actually it is made by huge machines in factories called power plants. It reaches our neighborhood through big metal wires, and then it travels down into our homes to wires inside our walls.

A substation. It changes the voltage of the electricity that comes from the power plant.

A transformer
It keeps electricity at the right voltage to use in our homes.

• To the Parent

Electrical power in most nations today is generated from three sources: water (hydroelectric) from dams or reservoirs; oil or coal boilers (thermal); and nuclear power. The amount generated by nuclear power is growing annually. Power systems differ by country, but in all countries plants transmit electricity in large units of kilovolts. These are reduced in local substations and again in neighborhood transformers to levels we use at home.

Ways to make electricity

Electricity is made by using some other type of power to run the machinery that makes the electricity. Usually it is water from a dam; or heat from coal, oil or the atom. But there are other ways, too.

▲ Big windmills, much larger than a house, can drive machines to make electricity.

▲ You know how hot the sun is. Mirrors can collect its heat to make electricity.

▲ Heat that comes from deep inside the earth can also be used to make electricity.

How Does a Thermos Work?

ANSWER Look in a thermos sometime. You'll see a mirror. Heat bounces off it and keeps liquid warm. Behind the mirror is a space without air. This also helps hold heat in the thermos.

Oof! I can't get out!
I just bounce back!
Hot water
Heat

How it works

▲ One bottle, two walls

The inside of the glass bottle is like a mirror, and heat bounces off of it. Also, the bottle has two walls, with no air in between. Heat can't leave without air to carry it.

Different Vacuum Jars

Jars for picnics

A rice cooker

An electric bottle

An Air-Pressure Flask

You can take water from some flasks just by pushing a button. That's because air is inside. When you push the button, the air has nowhere to go. So it squeezes down on the water, and pushes the water out through the spout.

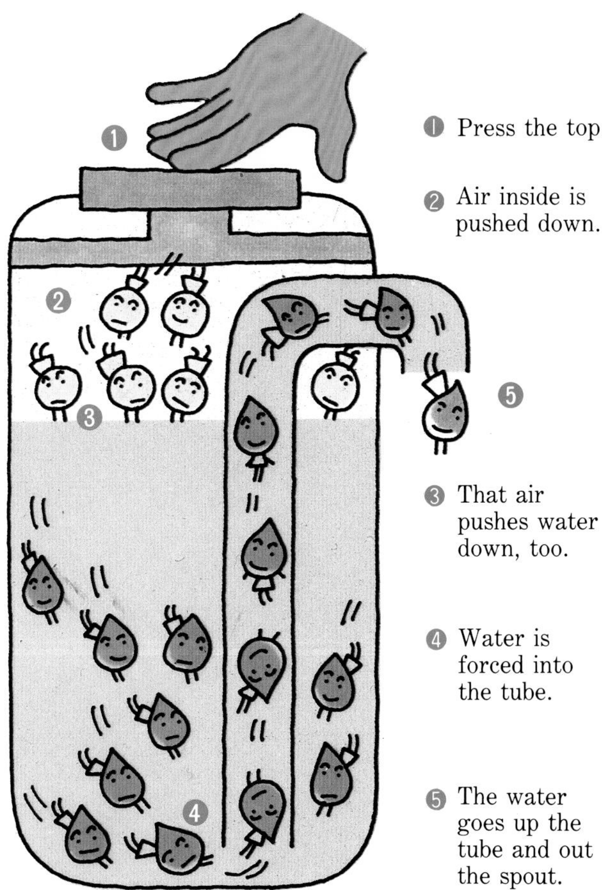

❶ Press the top.
❷ Air inside is pushed down.
❸ That air pushes water down, too.
❹ Water is forced into the tube.
❺ The water goes up the tube and out the spout.

TRY THIS

Cold things stay cold too

Fill a thermos with ice water and leave it. It stays cold for hours!

Wow! That's good and cold!

• To the Parent

Inside a vacuum flask is a double-wall glass jar. Its surface is metal-coated to make a mirror, which reflects the heat (or the cold) back inside. Between the walls there is no air, so heat won't transfer to the outside. Portable flasks may use plastic or metal instead of glass, so dropping or any other shocks won't break the jar. Vacuum flasks are normally used for liquids, but there are flasks that are made with wide mouths to carry hot or cold food.

Why Does Water Put Out a Fire?

ANSWER 1 For something to burn, it must be very, very hot. When water is poured on fire, the temperature drops instantly, and the fire quickly goes out.

The water's too cold! I'm dying out!

ANSWER 2 A fire also needs air to keep going. But there's no air in water, of course. So water keeps air away from the fire, and that's why the flames go out.

Oh, I can't breathe! I'm really done for!
Air

We can also use other things to put out a fire

Ooh! I can't go in there!

Powder or gas cuts off air

The tank is filled with liquid, gas or powder that doesn't burn. It is sprayed on the fire, and it cuts off air just as water does. We call the tanks fire extinguishers. They put out fire.

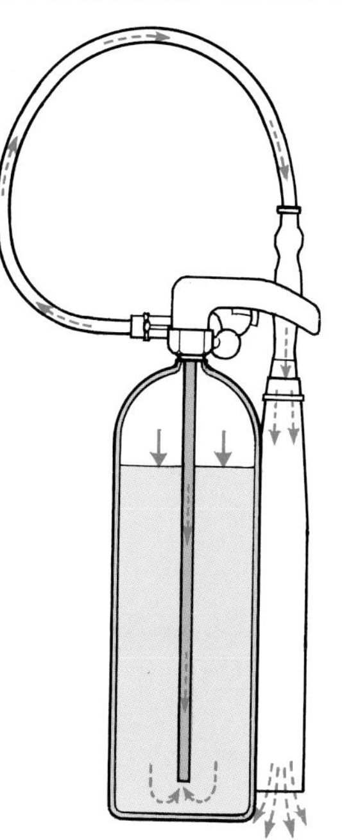

Extinguishers work differently. In this one gas forces a liquid out of the tube. The liquid then turns to foam, and that smothers the fire.

I'm sure glad the fire's out!

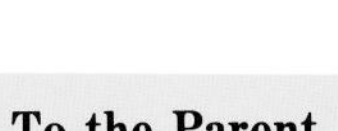

• To the Parent

To make things burn, high temperature and oxygen are needed. To put out a fire one of those elements must be removed. Water is good for fighting fire because it reduces the temperature sharply and cuts off the oxygen. It is not good for extinguishing oil fires, though, because oil floats on water, so water cannot cut off the oxygen supply. So we use foam, powder and carbon dioxide on oil fires. These cut off the oxygen.

Why Do Burning Things Make Smoke?

ANSWER When things burn, water in them and water vapor in the air get hot and form a kind of cloud. Mixed into it are bits of things that didn't burn in the fire. Together they make smoke.

When things burn...

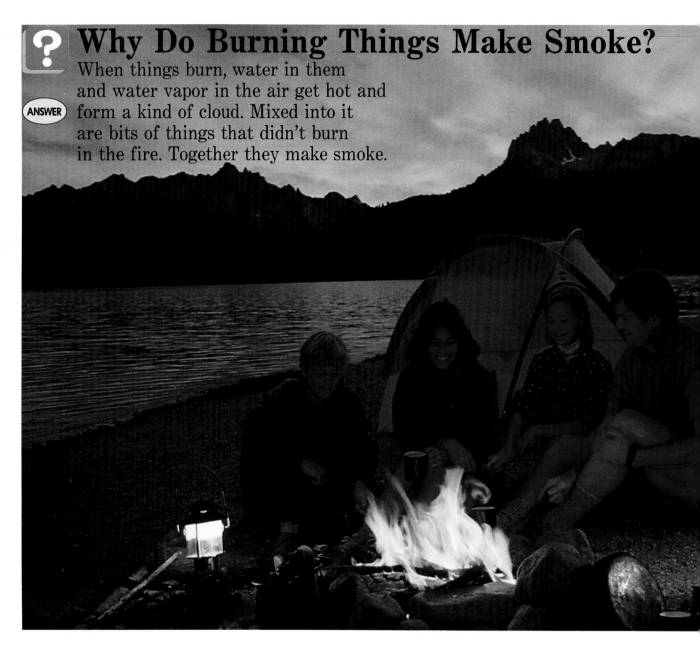

When a fire first starts to burn, there's a lot of smoke.

Once the fire catches, there is less and less smoke.

David Stoecklein/The Stock Market

How About Fires That Don't Smoke?

Fires make a lot of smoke only when they don't burn well. The water and the little unburned specks in smoke spread out and drift away in the air. Bigger specks fall back to the ground.

Smoke is made up of water vapor mixed with unburned specks that are so tiny you can't see them!

To the Parent

In a fire, the heated air sweeps water vapor, bits of the fuel that failed to burn and other matter up into the air. The vapor itself is invisible, but if it cools then it can be seen as droplets. These come together with other droplets and the bits, and make smoke. When a fire burns well even soot is consumed, so there is very little smoke. That's why a pan's bottom won't turn as black over a blue flame as it will over a yellow flame.

Why Won't Oil and Water Mix?

Some things mix easily with water. Oil weighs less than water, though, so instead of mixing it floats on water.

Water is heavier than oil. In the same jar water will always sink under the oil.

You can stir and stir, but the oil will always keep to itself, even in tiny bits.

TRY THIS

Oil keeps to itself in water

Put some oil and some water into a clean glass, and watch what happens when you stir them. Even though the oil breaks up into bits, the bits won't mix with the water.

When oil meets oil, they don't have any trouble mixing with each other.

Oil and water, though, aren't the same. Those two always separate.

Water and most things with water in them, like milk, mix very easily.

When you stop stirring, the bits of oil slowly start to move back together again.

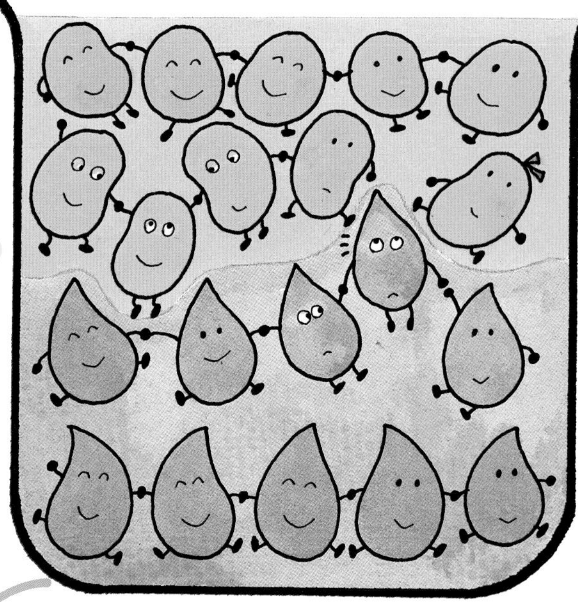

The oil rises back to the top, where it was, and soon both are separated again.

They're not very friendly.

• To the Parent

From edible oils to petroleum, oils come in various forms. You see them even in such solid fats as cheese and butter. But we generally use oil as the word for the liquid forms. Water and oil are made up of molecules that are not alike and will not link together, so oil and water do not mix. Further, oil is lighter than water, so it will always rise, even if you shake it very hard, and float on water.

Where Does Gasoline Come From?

ANSWER Gasoline is made from crude oil, which is pumped out of the ground. The crude oil is put through a special chemical process, which separates it into different kinds of fuels and oils. One of the fuels is the gasoline that cars and trucks use. At the gas station gasoline is stored in underground tanks. A hose is used to fill up your car's tank.

Gasoline Comes From a Big Oil Family

asoline is one of many fuels
ıat are made from oil. Each
ıel is made in its own way.
hese fuels have different
ames and different uses too.

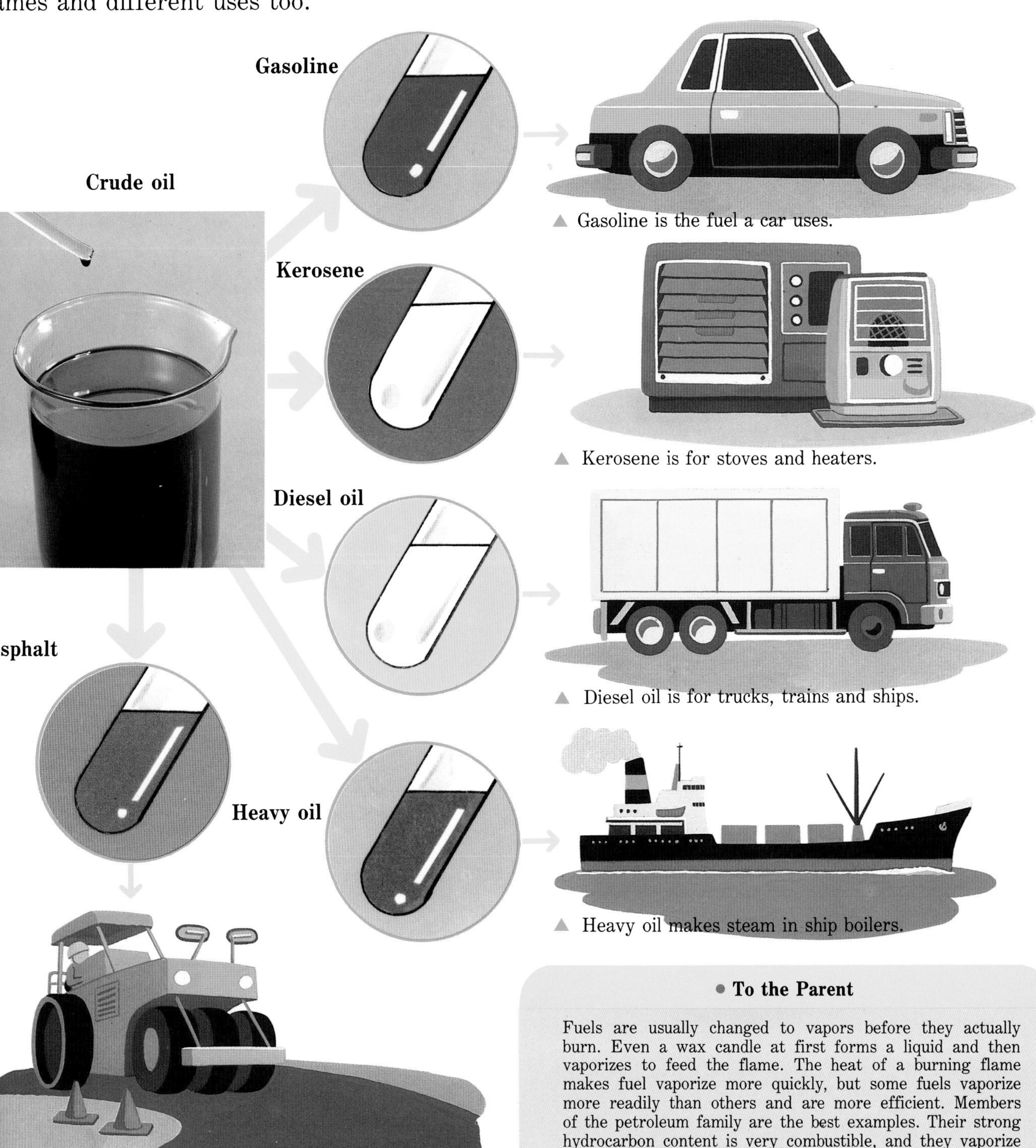

▲ Gasoline is the fuel a car uses.

▲ Kerosene is for stoves and heaters.

▲ Diesel oil is for trucks, trains and ships.

▲ Heavy oil makes steam in ship boilers.

▲ Asphalt covers roads all in black.

• To the Parent

Fuels are usually changed to vapors before they actually burn. Even a wax candle at first forms a liquid and then vaporizes to feed the flame. The heat of a burning flame makes fuel vaporize more quickly, but some fuels vaporize more readily than others and are more efficient. Members of the petroleum family are the best examples. Their strong hydrocarbon content is very combustible, and they vaporize well. Refining of crude oil into fuels takes advantage of the different vaporization temperature of fuels refined.

What Happens to Trash?

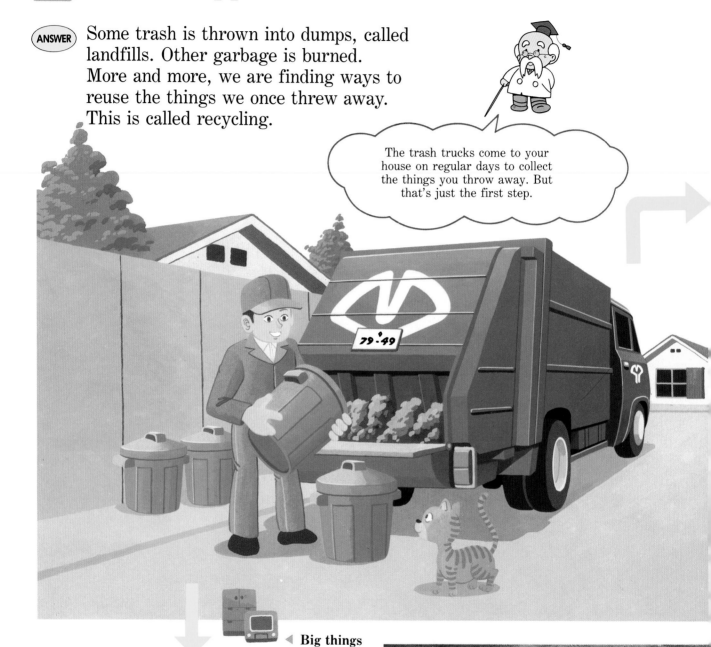

ANSWER Some trash is thrown into dumps, called landfills. Other garbage is burned. More and more, we are finding ways to reuse the things we once threw away. This is called recycling.

The trash trucks come to your house on regular days to collect the things you throw away. But that's just the first step.

Big things also go to landfills.

Landfill. At the end of each day the landfill is covered with dirt to keep out germs and animals.

Many Kinds of Trash Can Be Recycled

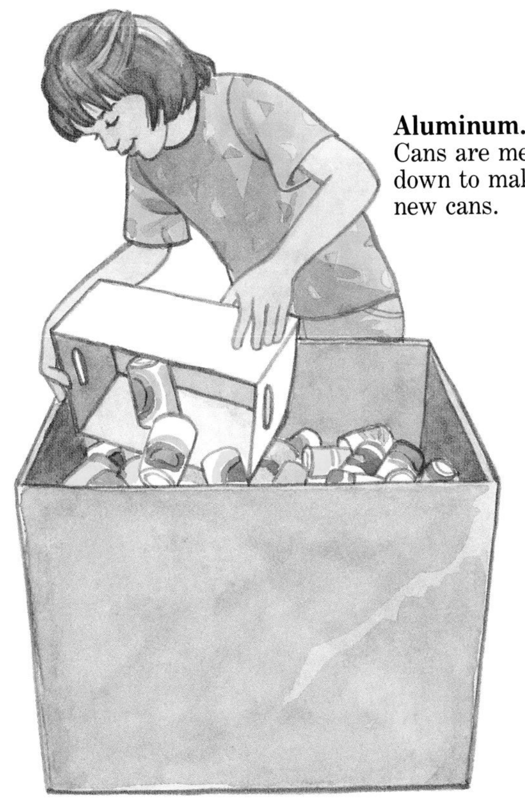

Aluminum. Cans are melted down to make new cans.

Glass. Bottles are turned into bricks, material for paving roads, or new bottles.

Paper. Old paper can be used to make new paper and boxes.

How Newspaper is Recycled

At paper mills, old newspapers are dumped into a huge machine that grinds them up and cooks them into a thick, paper soup called pulp. The pulp is pumped into other machines that wash it and bleach it white.

The clean, white pulp is then spread out onto a large screen that helps drain the water from it. Rollers squeeze out more water and dry the new paper. Finally, it is wound onto huge spools.

- **To the Parent**

Waste disposal varies from place to place according to need and available resources. Traditionally, trucks have hauled garbage to dumps and landfills. As dumps fill up, people have sought other methods of garbage disposal. More and more, communities have instituted mandatory recycling programs as a way of reducing their growing rubbish disposal burden.

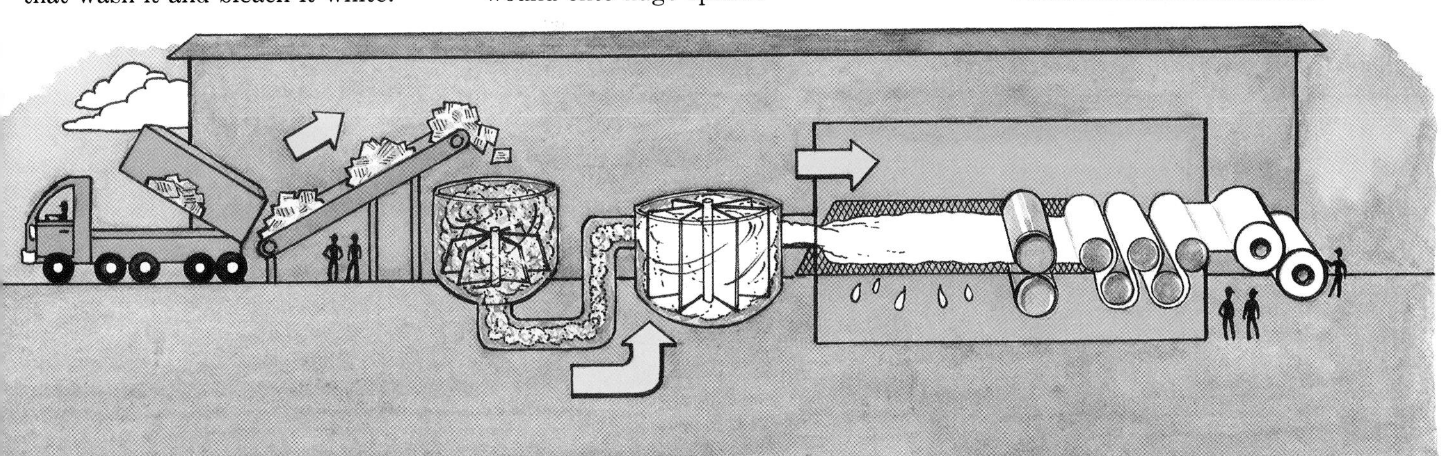

How Does a Telephone Work?

ANSWER When we talk into a phone it turns the sound of our voice into an electric signal. The signal travels over wires. At the other end another phone turns it back into sound.

Telephone office
Hello Grandma! Thank you for the cookies!
Electrical waves carry your voice.
TRY THIS
You can make your own telephone
Use a juice can or cardboard tube.
Cover the end with strong, thin paper and tape.
Of course I'm here!
Are you there?
Put string through the center and knot it tight.
Make the string about 15 feet (4.6 m) long. To talk, pull it tight and speak very loudly!

Thank you for the cookies!

How a telephone works

You hear the voice vibrations here.
And you speak into this end.

Here are some old ones

▲1897

▲1927

▲1950

▶Sidewalk telephone booth

A speaker on this office phone has a volume control.

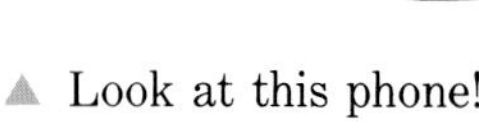

▲ Look at this phone!

• To the Parent

Sound is a phenomenon of vibration, and the telephone uses this principle to convert the vibrations of your voice into electrical signals that can travel over wire. A telephone actually has a small microphone in the speaking end of the handset and a tiny speaker in the earpiece. A phone call creates two circuits: microphone to speaker at each end. Many new refinements are being added; we already talk by satellite, and soon our voices will travel on light waves.

How Does a TV Work?

ANSWER TV signals are sent through the air as electrical waves. TV antennas catch the waves, and TV sets change them into sound and pictures.

TV antenna

3. TV tower
This tower makes the pictures into waves and sends them out.

4. TV set
It makes the waves back into pictures again by using light to draw them all on the screen quickly.

Tiny TVs

A head-set model

To the Parent

Television is a complicated technology that has become part of our daily lives. The camera-broadcast source breaks down light into FM radio waves, which are then transmitted to the home from the TV station's tower. The television tube makes them back into pictures by shooting electron beams at its surface from behind. These strike phosphor bits all over the screen, lighting them up. The action comes from showing a series of still pictures very fast, a bit like movie film.

1. TV studio
In the studio a big camera first turns the picture into electricity. Sounds go with it over wires from the studio through a large control room.

2. Control room
Here the pictures from many cameras are controlled, and the best ones are picked to turn into waves that can be sent over the air.

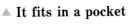

▲ **It fits in a pocket**

▲ **An inside view of the wiring**

How Does a Piano Make Music?

ANSWER Inside the piano are 88 strings made of steel. When you strike a key, it makes a hammer hit a string. That makes the sound.

Inside the piano

Strings
Different sizes and lengths. Different sounds!

Hammers
Press the keys, and hammers tap the strings.

▲ The hammers are covered with felt.

How a piano makes notes of music

When a hammer taps a string, the string vibrates and makes a sound. That's called a note. Each string is a different size, so each makes a different note. We play many notes together to make music.

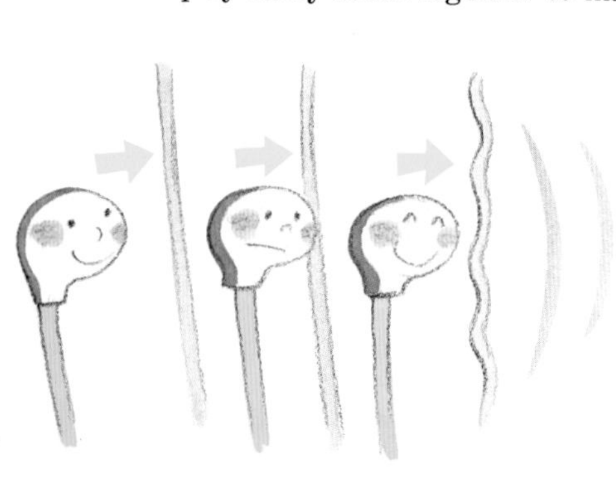

How Do Other Instruments Make Their Own Sounds?

▶ **Guitar.** These strings are strummed with your fingers.

▲ **Xylophone.** When you hit a key it vibrates to make a note.

▲ **Drum.** When the tight skin is hit it makes a noise.

▲ **Glasses.** With different water levels, their sounds differ.

▲ **Rubber band.** Twang a rubber band: it makes a funny sort of sound.

◀ **Violin.** The strings make sounds from the bow scraping on them.

▲ **Whistle.** It's your own mouth. It makes air vibrate to make notes!

◀ **Flute.** With this, the air vibrates inside the instrument. Your fingers make the notes.

▲ **Harmonica.** When you blow, thin metal plates inside vibrate to make notes.

• To the Parent

Sound, as we saw with the telephone, comes from vibration. The vibration is transmitted through the air and strikes our eardrums to make them vibrate also. This is what we detect as music when we hear an instrument or a song. Musical instruments are divided into various types, depending on how the vibration is made: by striking, strumming, scraping or blowing. The sound is deeper when the source (e.g., a piano string) is thick or long, and higher when it is thin or short.

How Does a Record Make Sounds?

ANSWER If you look closely at a record you'll see many tiny grooves. These grooves are a kind of code. A record player is made to read the code and turn it into music.

A record's grooves

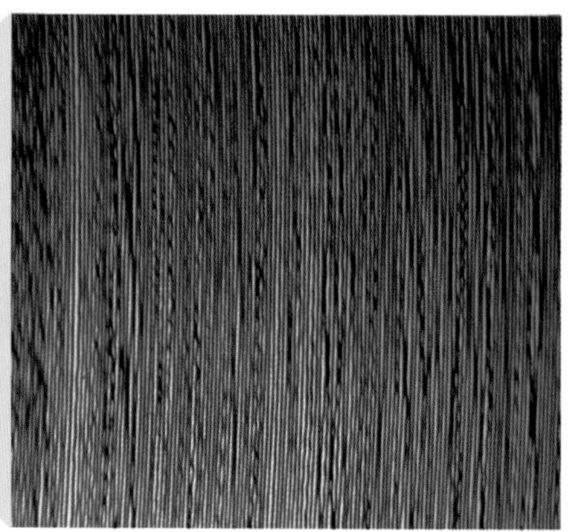

▲ **A close-up look at the grooves**

The lines you can see on records are called grooves. They contain all the information that a record player needs to make music.

How a record player works

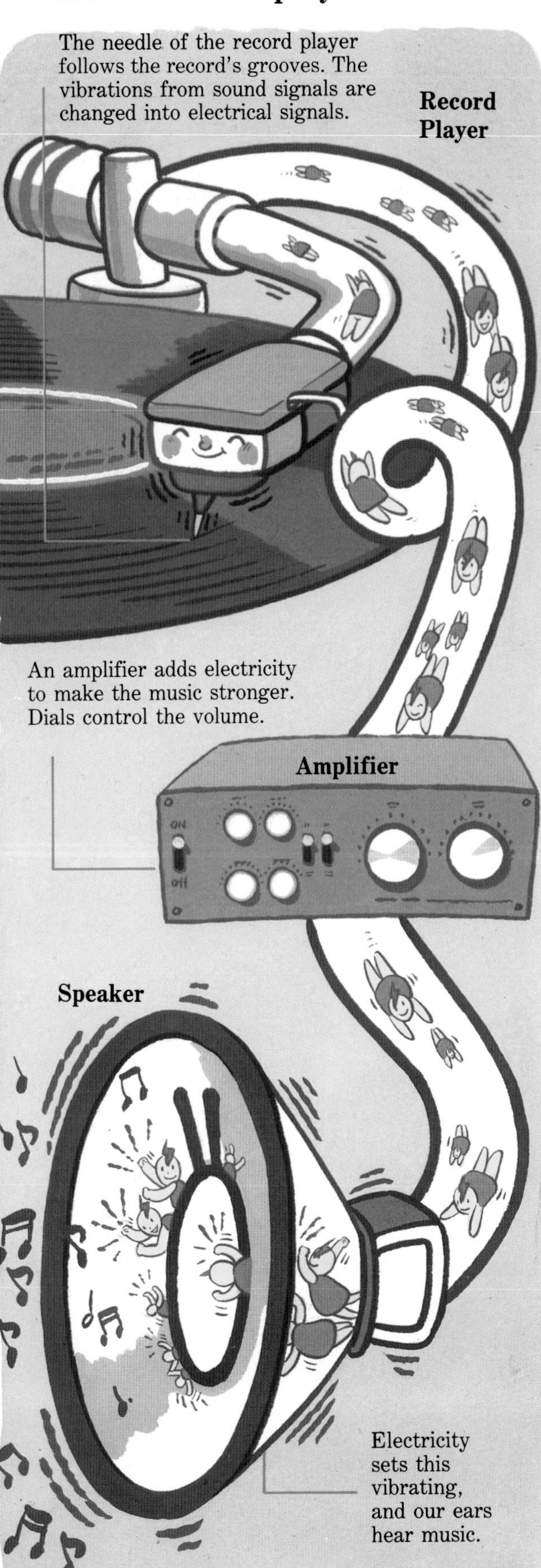

The needle of the record player follows the record's grooves. The vibrations from sound signals are changed into electrical signals.
Record Player
An amplifier adds electricity to make the music stronger. Dials control the volume.
Amplifier
ON
off
Speaker
Electricity sets this vibrating, and our ears hear music.

Pictures on Records

A laser disc is like a record but makes sound and pictures too.

▲ **The disc has grooves too small to see**

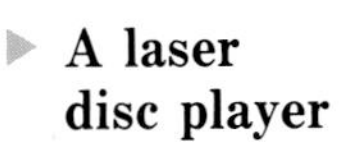

▶ **A laser disc player**

• To the Parent

When a record is made, sound recorded on tape is converted to the vibration of a needle and the vibrations are etched as bumps into the groove of a master record. Copies, made primarily of vinyl chloride, are pressed from this master, and the needle of your phonograph then reconverts them to vibrations. Lasers can record sound and images on a coded disc. This information is later translated into audio and video signals to be played back on a television receiver.

How Are Pencils Made?

ANSWER A chemical called graphite is mixed with clay to make pencil lead. The pencil lead is then put inside a long holder made of wood.

Making pencils

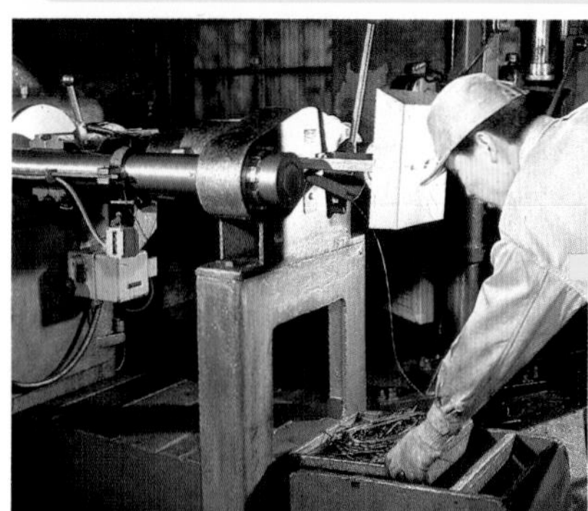

▲ First graphite is made into powder and mixed with clay. A machine shapes the mix to turn it into a pencil lead.

▲ The leads are cut into pieces as long as pencils and dried. The dried leads are then baked to make them hard.

▲ A long piece of wood is cut with a groove, and the lead fits right in. Another piece of wood is glued on top of it.

Pencil Leads Can Be Made Hard or Soft, Thick or Thin

Pencils with soft, thick leads make dark marks and are used to draw pictures.

Pencils that have medium softness and thickness in leads are used for writing.

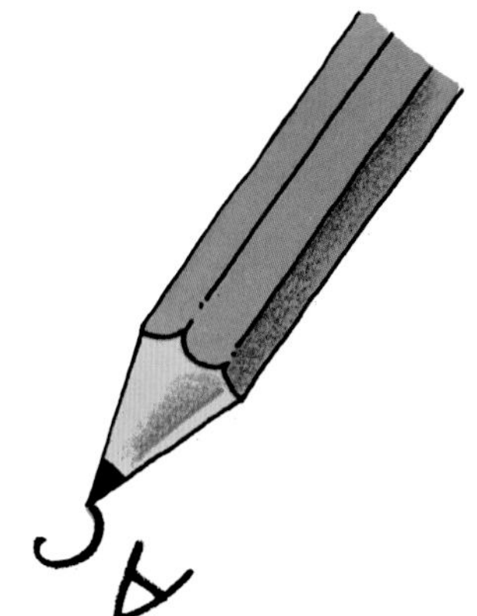

Pencils with thin, hard leads are used to draw such things as designs.

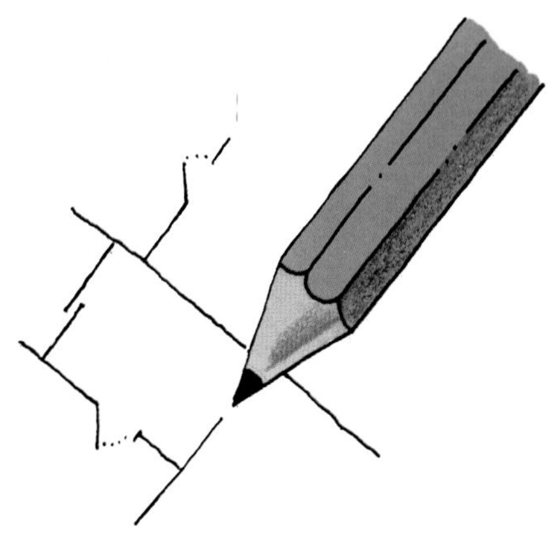

Pencils of all kinds

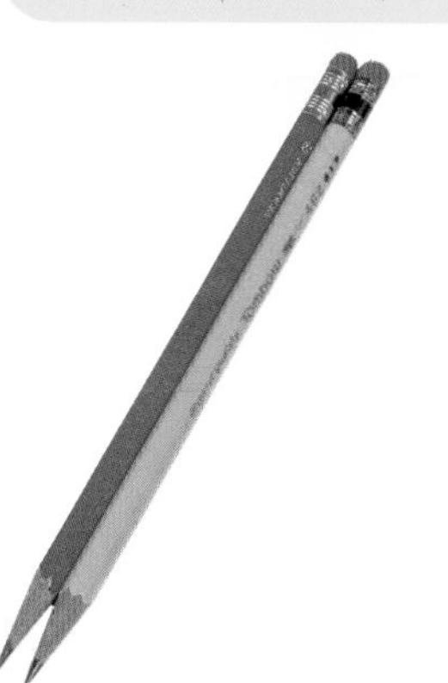

▲ Some have erasers attached.

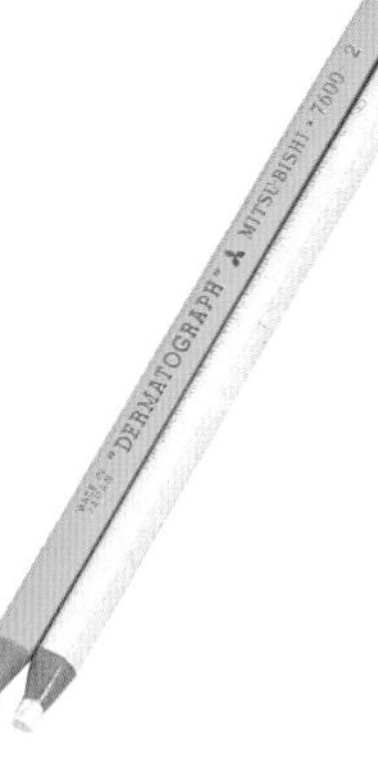

▲ Some don't even have real leads.

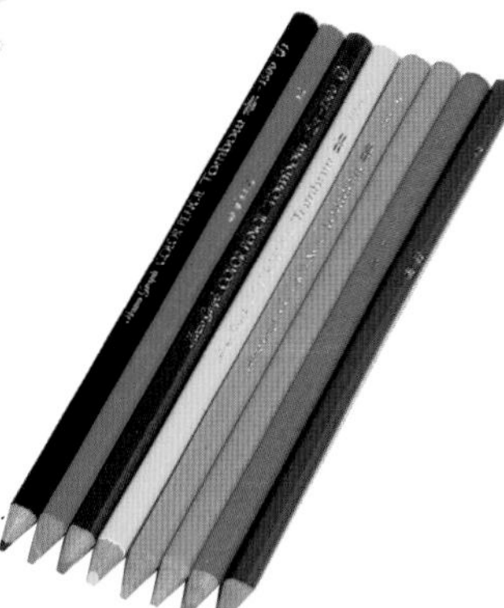

▲ Some sets have many colors.

▲ Some are made with flat points.

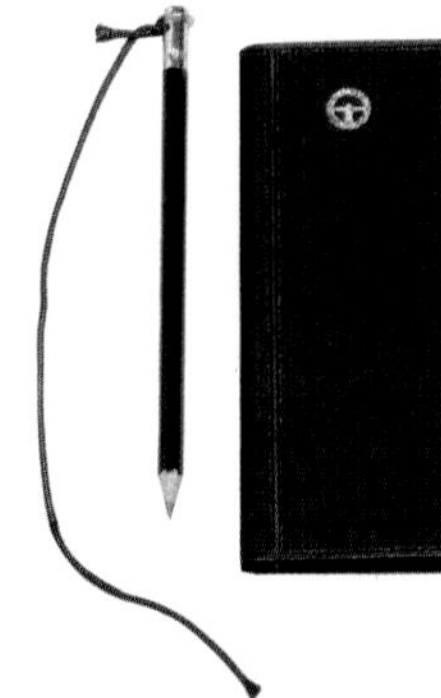

▲ Some are made for notebooks.

▲ The wood is then shaved flat or rounded smoothly on all sides, paint is added, and the pencil is finished!

Letters and designs can be added when the paint goes on.

• To the Parent

Pencils are made in many gradations of hardness, from very soft and black to extremely hard and not very black. The degree of hardness is shown by a letter or a number or by a combination of letters and numbers. Harder leads have more clay and soft ones have a greater amount of graphite. Colored leads are white clay and dye.

How Does an Air Conditioner Cool a Room?

ANSWER The air conditioner pulls warm air inside it, removes all the heat from the air and sends cooled air into the house. The heat is sent out the window. An air conditioner is made specially to do this over and over.

How air is cooled

Air conditioners use a special gas that changes back and forth from a liquid to a gas very easily. But each time it goes back to a gas, it takes heat out of the air. It uses a process that we call evaporation.

What Makes the Inside of the Refrigerator Stay Cold?

A refrigerator works the same way. It keeps the cold air inside. The heat is sent out through coils in the back.

Freezer section. Here's where you make ice and keep your ice cream!
Evaporator This takes out heat and makes the air inside the refrigerator colder.
Egg rack
Cheese and butter holders
Refrigeration area
Shelves to hold milk, bottles and other things
Compressor This part squeezes the gas so it becomes a liquid once again.

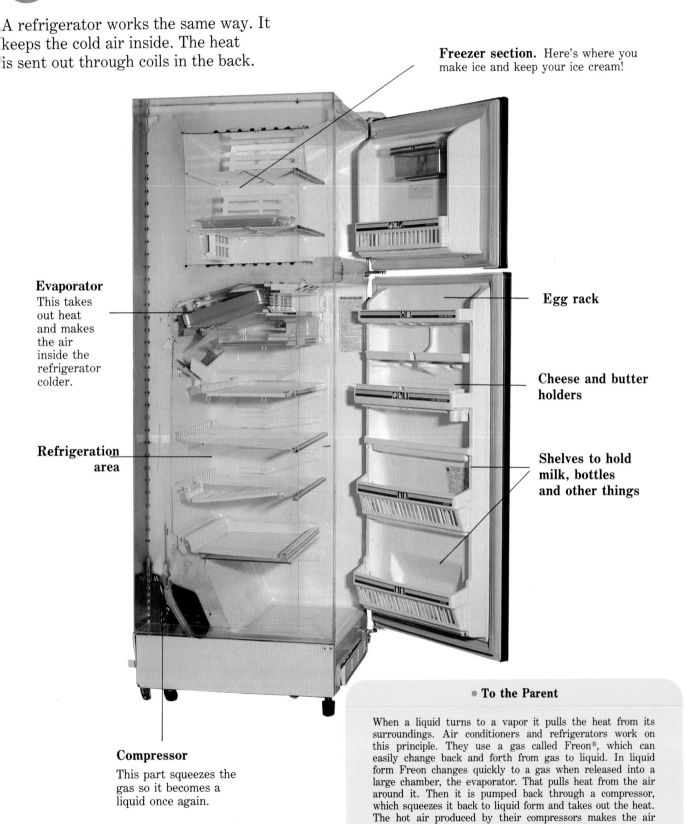

• To the Parent

When a liquid turns to a vapor it pulls the heat from its surroundings. Air conditioners and refrigerators work on this principle. They use a gas called Freon®, which can easily change back and forth from gas to liquid. In liquid form Freon changes quickly to a gas when released into a large chamber, the evaporator. That pulls heat from the air around it. Then it is pumped back through a compressor, which squeezes it back to liquid form and takes out the heat. The hot air produced by their compressors makes the air conditioner and the back of a refrigerator discharge heat.

Why Does a Fan Make a Breeze?

ANSWER The fan has blades that are slanted, not flat. When they turn very quickly, they blow the air at us.

■ How a fan makes the air move

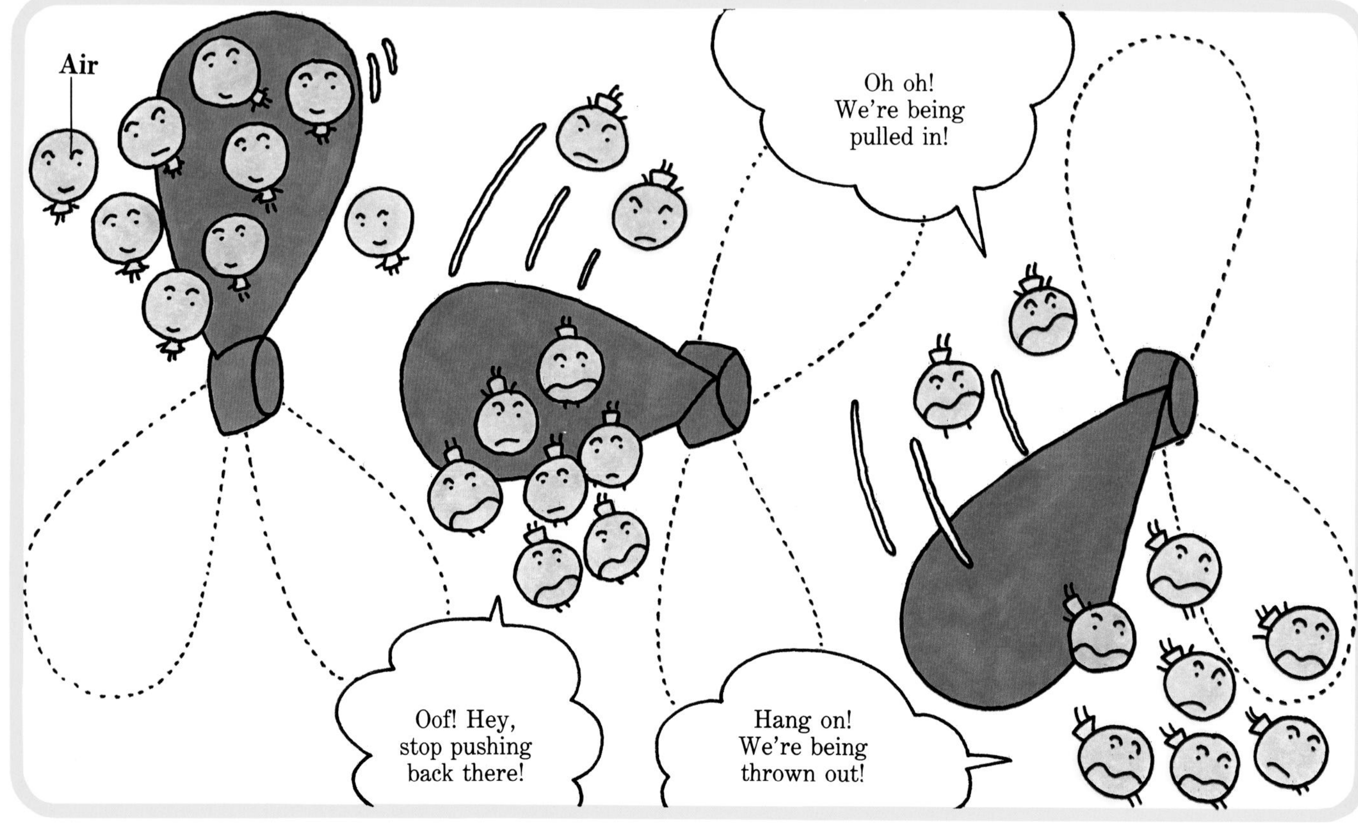

Different Fans Can Make Air Do All Kinds of Work

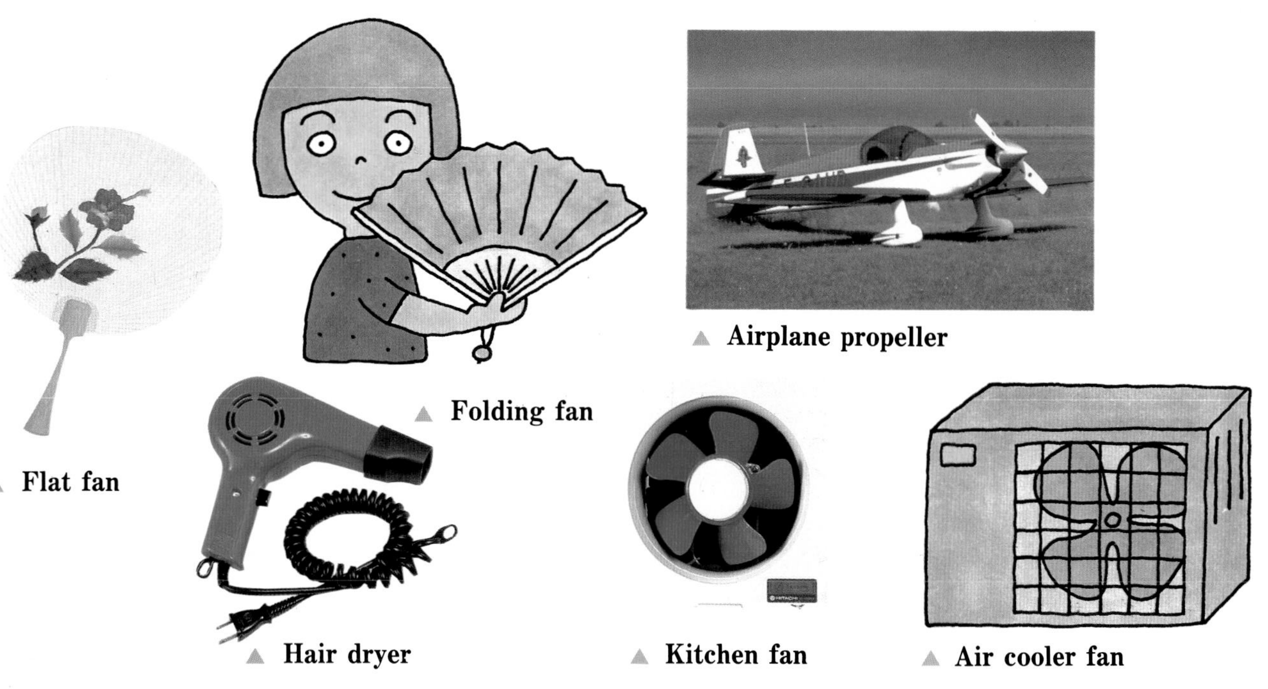

Why Does a Breeze Make Us Feel Cooler?

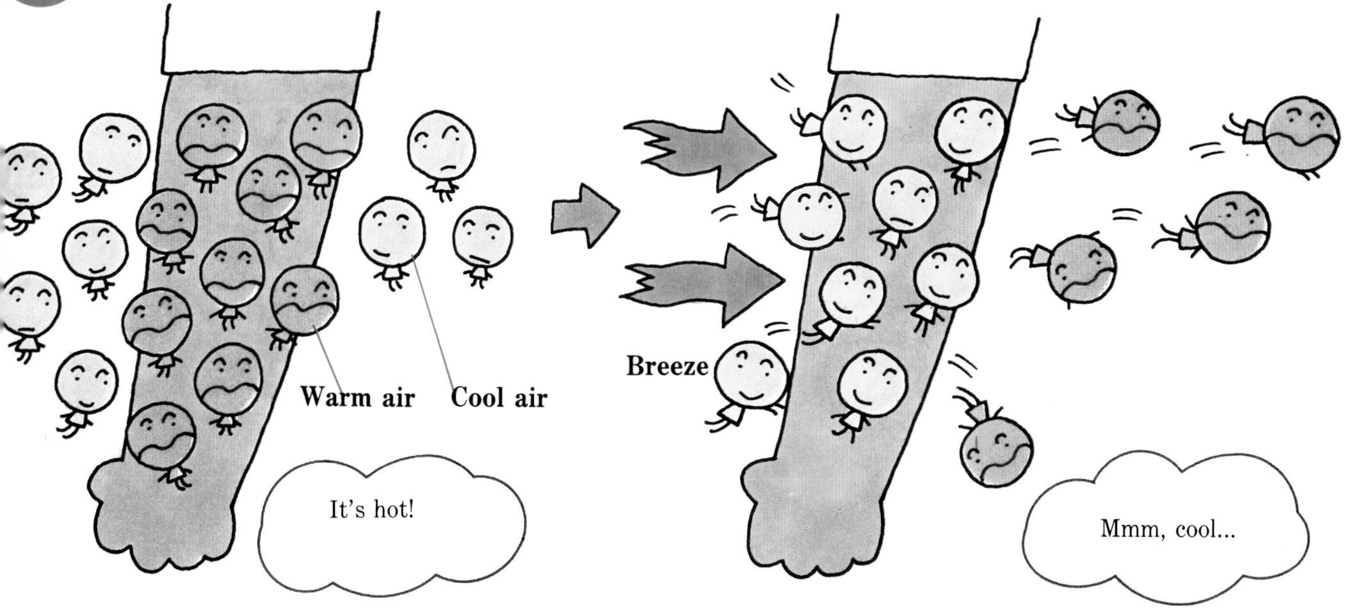

'hen there is no breeze, the air that ırrounds our bodies gets just as hot as ır bodies themselves. On a hot day, ıat doesn't feel good. A breeze blows ıis hot air away from us, and air that cooler takes its place. That's why a 'eeze feels so good to us when it's hot.

• To the Parent

The electric fan produces a breeze because of the way its blades are curved. The angle of the blade's face will push air out; and of course the higher the speed, the more air is sucked in from behind and pushed out to the front. Airplane propellers work on this principle, but in reverse. You can demonstrate this with a hand-held fan: if its flat side is facing you, moving it side to side will produce no breeze. Angling one side 45° toward you will produce a nice breeze.

Why Can't We See Clearly Through Frosted Glass?

ANSWER The glass is rough on one side so light can't go straight through. If light is mixed up, the things we see are too.

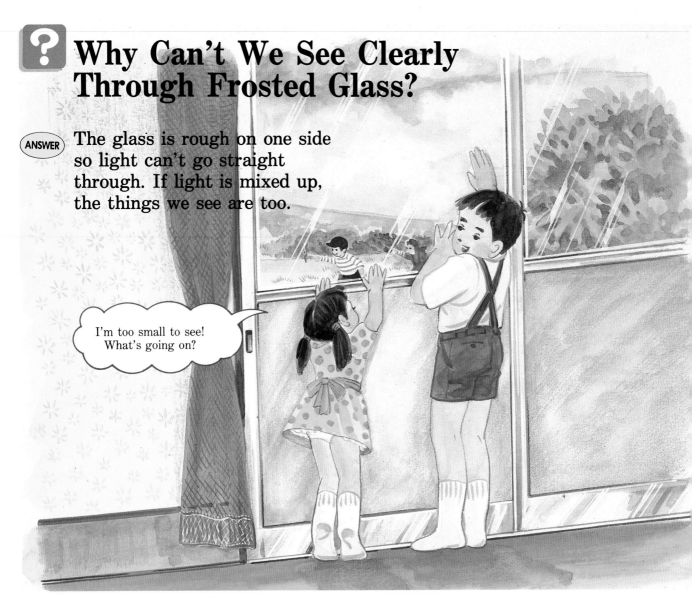

I'm too small to see!
What's going on?

How light goes through frosted glass

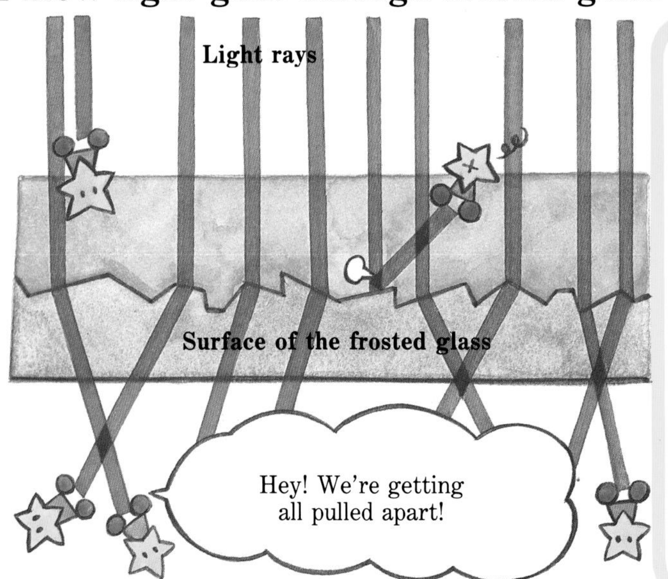

TRY THIS

Making frosted glass clear

Take a wet rag, and very slowly wipe the rough side of the glass so that water clings to it.

Look closely at the wet parts, and you'll be able to see! It's because the water fills in the roughness, making a flat surface again.

How Do They Make Frosted Glass?

The surface of frosted glass is made rough by putting many small scratches on it. They are made by blowing tiny bits of sand at a high speed against one side of the glass.

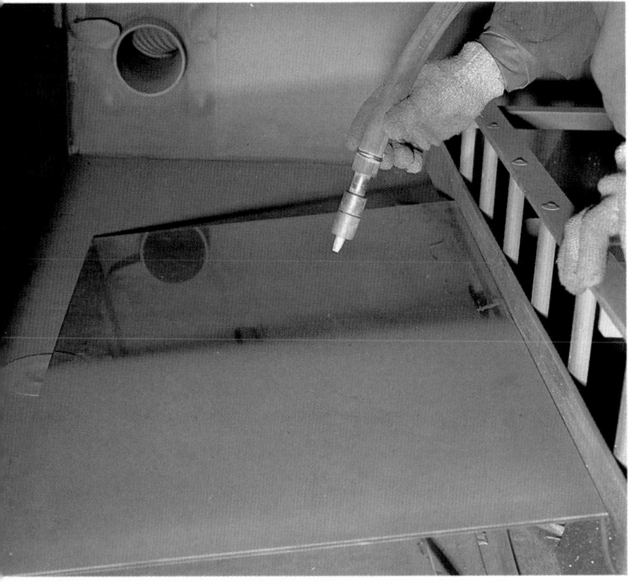

▲ This worker is making frosted glass by spraying sand. The white part is already finished.

The reason light bulbs are white is that they are frosted too. Bulbs are treated with chemicals, however, rather than sand.

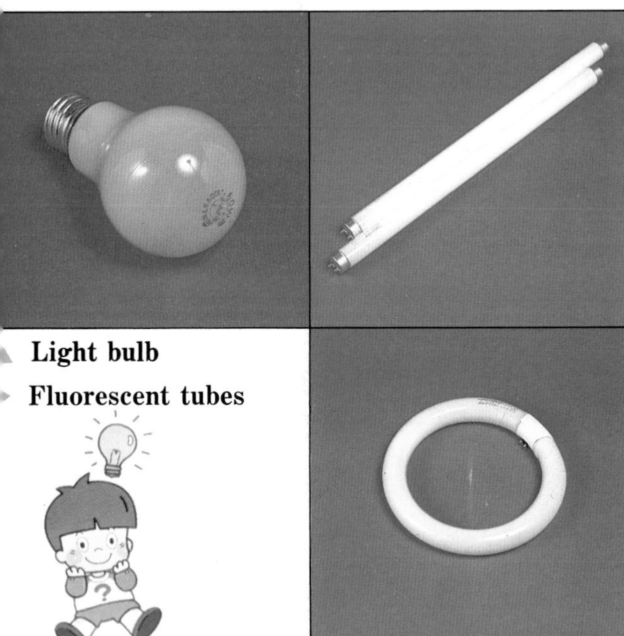

▲ Light bulb

▸ Fluorescent tubes

Many Pretty Patterns

▲ Designs are drawn with blowing sand

▲ Colored glass

▲ Glass with wires

◂ Glass that looks like a mirror

• To the Parent

Transparent glass allows rays of light to pass through it without bending, and the images they carry are seen clearly. The unevenness of frosted glass directs the rays into random patterns, so images cannot be seen distinctly. Frosted glass was formerly made by placing tiny bits of hard sand on the surface itself, but today machines blow the sand over the surface to erode it. Light bulbs and other small items are frosted with hydrogen fluoride, a gas that corrodes glass.

Why Do We Stir Bath Water?

ANSWER Water on top is hotter than water down below. So we have to stir to make sure they mix well.

OH BOY! THAT'S JUST RIGHT!
YOW!! THAT WATER'S FREEZING

What happened? The hot water at the top felt good. But the rest, at the bottom, was still cold.

Hot and cold water

As water is heated it expands like anything else. That makes it lighter, which means it floats upward just like a big hot-air balloon. In the bathtub it all collects at the top. Water that's not as hot stays heavy and sinks down to the bottom. That means that before you get in you have to stir.

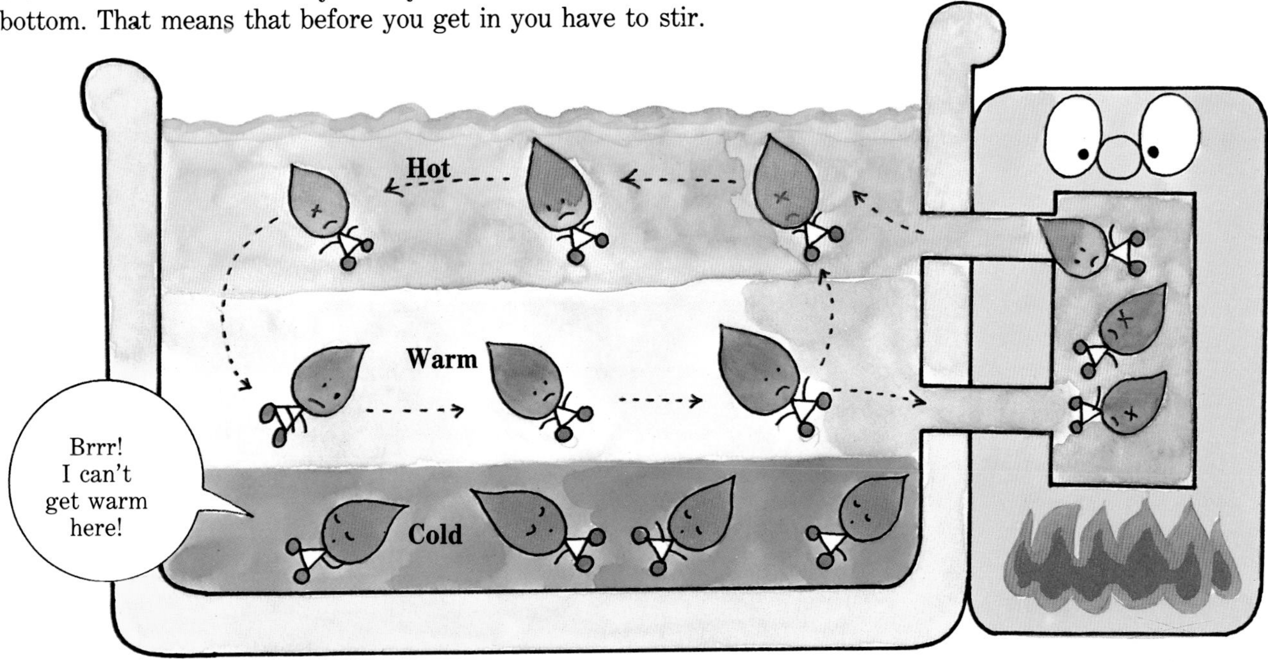

TRY THIS

Warm air gets lighter

In a room with one heater, the warm air gets lighter and goes up to the ceiling quickly. Cool air sinks down to the floor. If you stand on something high you'll feel warmer.

• To the Parent

When water and air are heated they expand and become less dense than an equal volume that is cold. For that reason, warm air weighs less than the same quantity of cold air or water, and warm is pushed upward as the cold sinks. This process is called convection, and it is why the condenser, or cooling part, of a refrigerator is at the top. This is also why an air conditioner is placed high inside a room.

Why Do Bathroom Windows Steam Up?

ANSWER 1 Some of the bath water gets so hot it turns into a gas called water vapor, which floats up to the window. If the glass is cold from outside air it cools the vapor and turns it back into water.

TRY THIS

Water drops make the glass steamy

Wipe your hand over a steamy window. Feel how cool it is.

Vapor that the glass has cooled will come off as drops of water.

Water vapor changes back to water when it's cool

Wow!
It's cold
up here!
When water
vapor gets
cool it
changes to
tiny drops
of water.

ANSWER 2

The window steams up because hot bath water changes to vapor. Vapor keeps on forming. After a while there's so much of it that it sticks to the glass and makes it fog up.

HOT!
Ow!
It's so
hot!

• To the Parent

Water vapor, including steam, is a gas and is invisible. That white color you see in steam is really tiny droplets of water already cooling back down to a liquid. Windows in the bath are cooled by outside air, and that condenses the bath vapors into water. Rain is made the same way as is the "fog" in the bathroom. Water is evaporated by sunlight, rises, cools high up in the atmosphere and then condenses into raindrops.

Why Does Soap Take Dirt Out So Easily?

ANSWER Some dirt has oil in it. Water won't mix with oil. But soap mixes with both, so it lets water wash away oil.

Soap pulls out dirt

Hey, you!
Let me go!
No! Get out!
I'm washed up!

▲ Soap mixes with water and finds the dirt.

▲ The soap surrounds the dirt spot and pulls it apart.

▲ In tiny bits the oily dirt washes away in the water.

TRY THIS

Oil and water mix

Most dirt will wash away with water. But not oily dirt. You can see how soap makes the oil go by mixing them in clear water.

◀ Pour about half a glass of warm water, and put in a little salad oil. See how the oil floats on top of the water?

◀ Scrape off a few flakes of soap, put them in and stir very well.

◀ The soap breaks the oil down into tiny, tiny bits. These mix with the water, making it cloudy.

Different Kinds of Soap

Hand soap for your skin

Kitchen soap for dishes

Laundry soap for clothes

• To the Parent

Most dirt that cannot be washed away with ordinary water is oil-based; it won't mix. Soap has a chemical structure that will dissolve in water and penetrate oil to break it into very tiny bits. This both dissolves the dirt and makes the oil capable of mixing into the water so it can be flushed away. Waterfowl depend on the same oil-water principle to stay afloat on the surface. Their feathers are coated with natural oil. In soapy water they would lose the oil and sink.

How Does a Washing Machine Clean Clothes?

ANSWER 1 Look closely at your clothes. See all the tiny threads? Dirt gets in between them and is hard to get out. Blades in the washer's tub move the clothes back and forth, so soapy water mixes among all the threads, pushing the dirt out.

This blade spins back and forth.

▲ **Inside a washer**

The blades at the bottom push soapy water and clothes around and around. The blades turn one way, then the other way!

▲ **The water goes around and around**

ANSWER 2 The soap you put in the wash water loosens dirt in the clothes. Then the water can carry it down the drain.

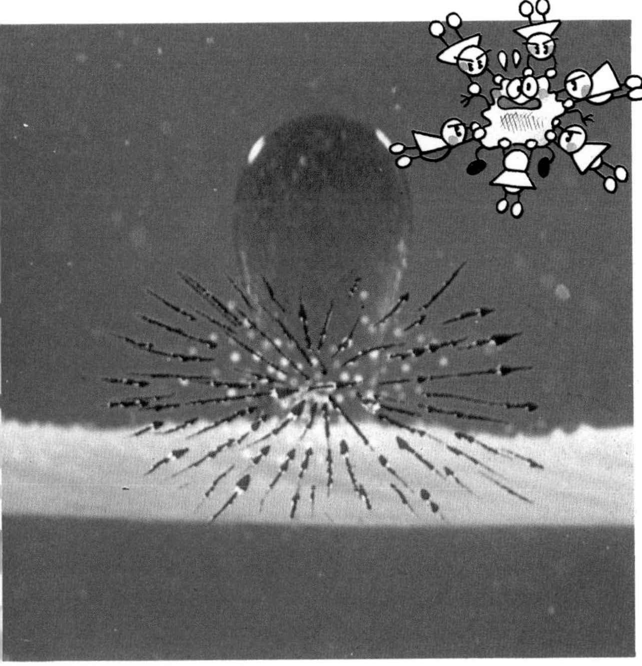

▲ Here's the soap at work. See how it surrounds bits of dirt, and pulls them from the cloth?

Here's a BIG washing machine

This one is for a laundry and can wash a lot of clothes at one time.

Ways to Wash Clothes

▶ **Treading.** Water is poured on the clothes, and the dirt is loosened by stamping.

▶ **Flailing.** After clothes are soaked in water they're slapped over a rock to loosen the dirt in them.

▶ **Scrubbing.** In a tub of hot, soapy water, clothes are rubbed on a wash-board to loosen the dirt.

• To the Parent

Oil-based dirt cannot be removed with water alone. Soap acts as a catalyst, which breaks down the oil into bits that can be washed away. Clothing has an added problem: dirt becomes ground into the weave of the fabric and is hard to remove. Thus washing clothes has always taken a lot of hard labor. The dirt must be loosened by striking, rubbing or twisting the fabric so water can work its way in. The washing machine has made this hard process much easier.

How Do Erasers Remove Writing?

ANSWER Pencils make marks with bits of lead left on the paper. But those bits stick to the eraser and come off with it.

How pencil drawings are rubbed away with an eraser

The pencil leaves a trail of tiny bits of its lead.

▲ The eraser rubber is soft: the lead sticks to it.

▲ Bits of eraser, black with lead, fall onto the paper.

But Erasers Don't Work With Things Drawn in Ink or Crayon — Why Is That?

Crayons use colored wax to make marks, and it sticks to the paper. So erasers can't rub it off.

Ink is a liquid, and it soaks into the paper. So rubbing the paper with an eraser won't take it out.

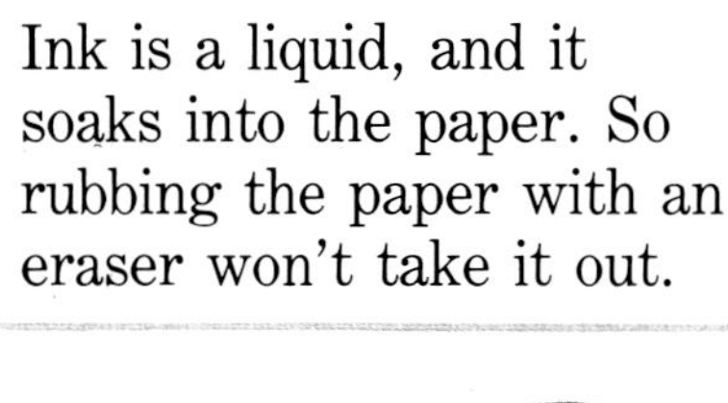

Types of erasers

▲ A plain eraser

▲ Erasers attached to pencil ends

▲ This eraser is shaped like a pencil

▲ Even erasers with pictures

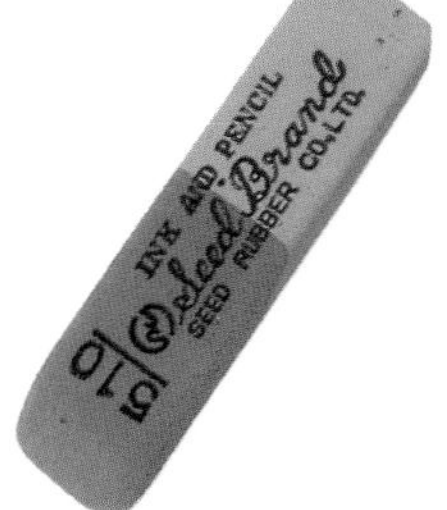

▲ Ink erasers have sand for rubbing

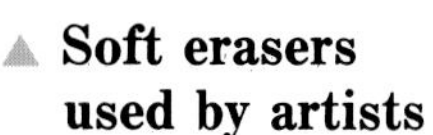

▲ Soft erasers used by artists

• To the Parent

The marks a pencil makes are powdered bits of its lead that are ground off by the pressure of writing and stick lightly to the paper. The eraser is soft enough that its surface is sticky. Rubbing it across the marks both picks up the lead powder and scrapes off the bits of the eraser to which they stick. The eraser is self-cleaning. Most erasers today are made of synthetics. An ink eraser contains very fine sand. It has to rub off the ink-soaked surface of the paper itself.

Why Does Rubber Stretch And Then Shrink?

ANSWER Rubber is a material that stretches easily because its tiniest parts, called molecules, change shape easily. When rubber shrinks, the molecules return to their normal shape.

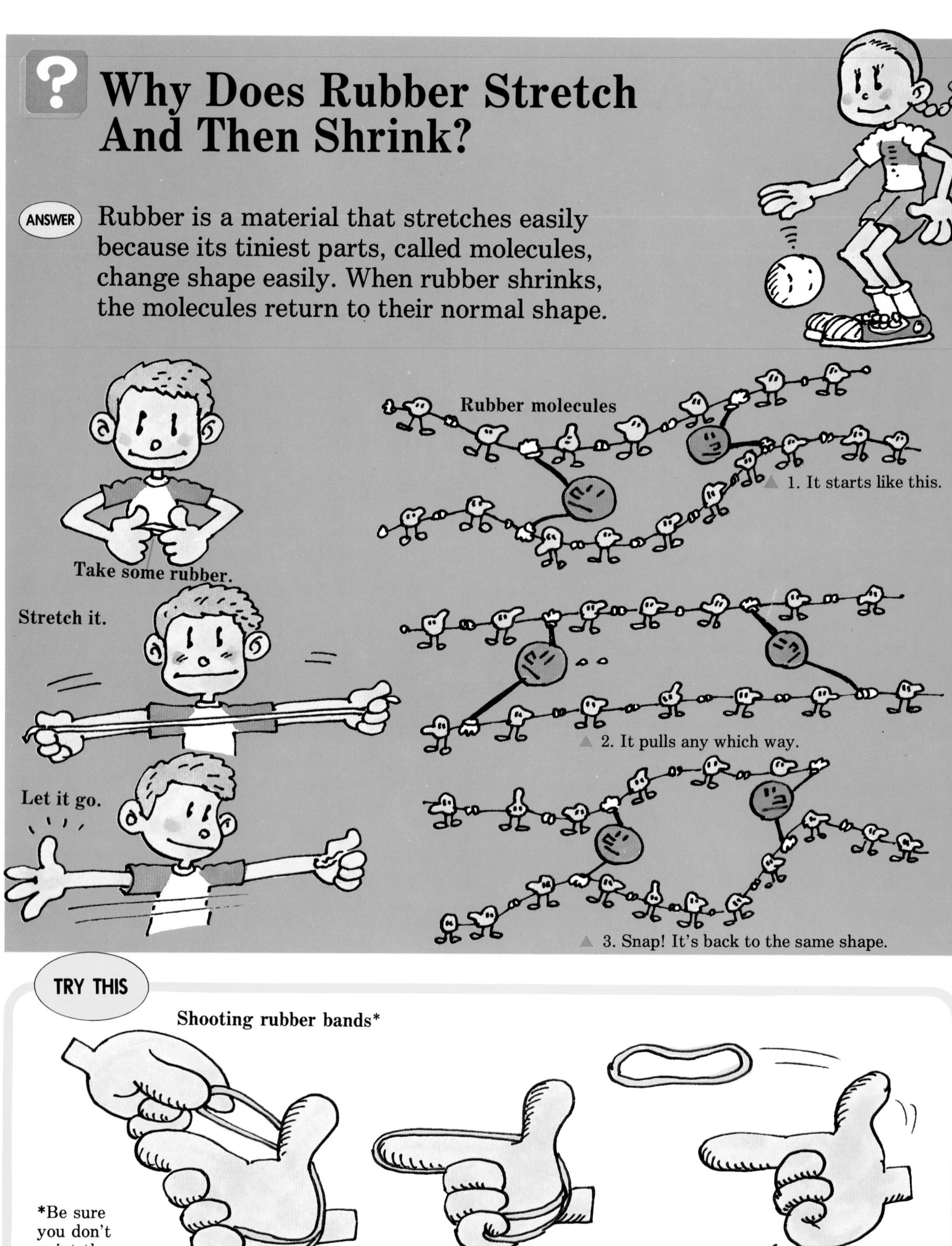
Take some rubber.
Stretch it.
Let it go.
Rubber molecules
1. It starts like this.
2. It pulls any which way.
3. Snap! It's back to the same shape.
TRY THIS
Shooting rubber bands*
*Be sure you don't point them at anyone!
Hold the rubber band this way...
And let your little finger go!

Making Rubber

▲ **Rubber trees.** If you cut the bark, a white sap flows out. It is collected in buckets. This sap is made into many rubber products.

▲ **A tire factory.** Other things are put into the sap to make it stronger. It's rolled out in big strips, then cut to make tires.

Things made of rubber

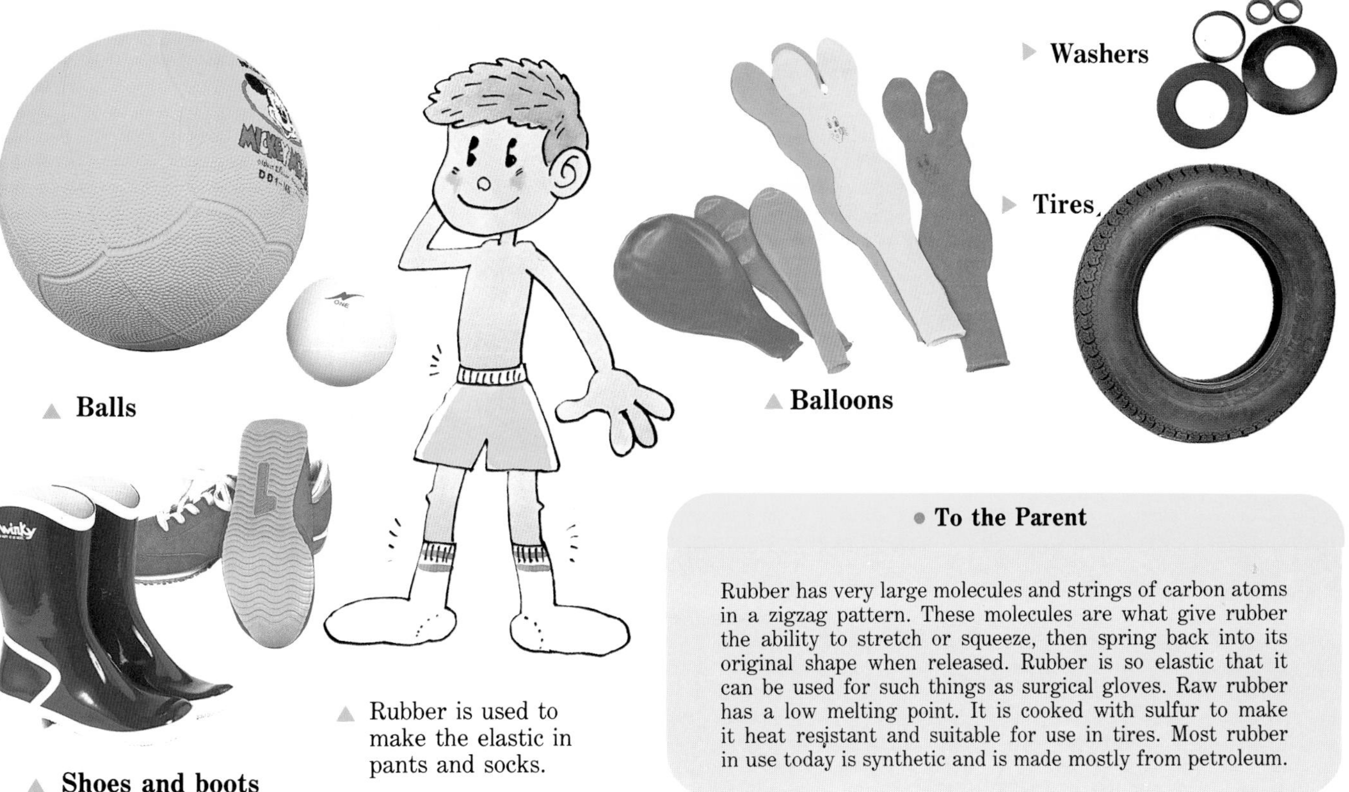

▲ **Balls**

▶ **Washers**

▶ **Tires**

▲ **Balloons**

▲ **Shoes and boots**

▲ Rubber is used to make the elastic in pants and socks.

• To the Parent

Rubber has very large molecules and strings of carbon atoms in a zigzag pattern. These molecules are what give rubber the ability to stretch or squeeze, then spring back into its original shape when released. Rubber is so elastic that it can be used for such things as surgical gloves. Raw rubber has a low melting point. It is cooked with sulfur to make it heat resistant and suitable for use in tires. Most rubber in use today is synthetic and is made mostly from petroleum.

Why Does Steel Rust?

ANSWER Steel is very strong. But when it is mixed with air and water it will rust.

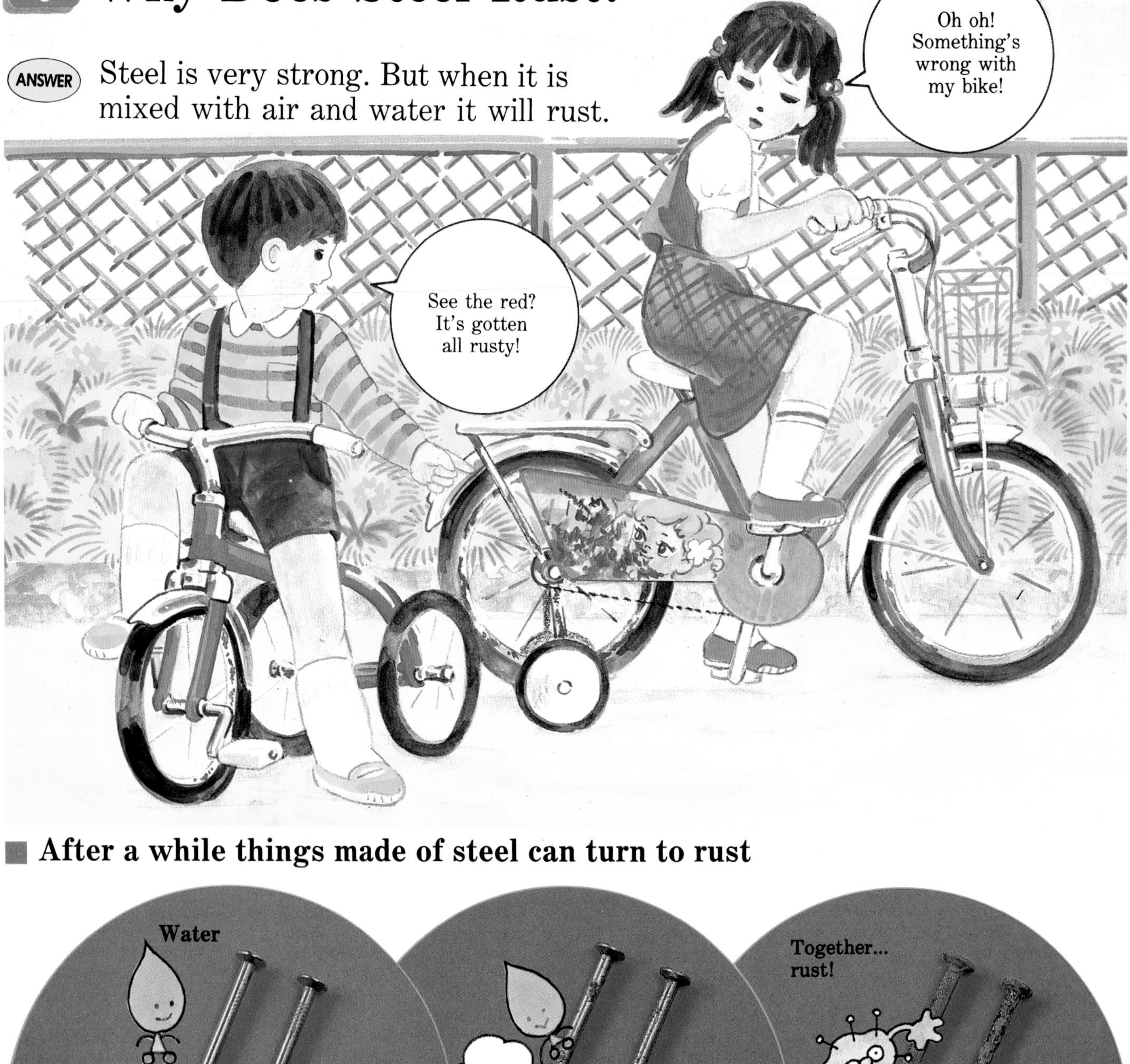

Oh oh! Something's wrong with my bike!
See the red? It's gotten all rusty!

After a while things made of steel can turn to rust

Water
Air
Together... rust!

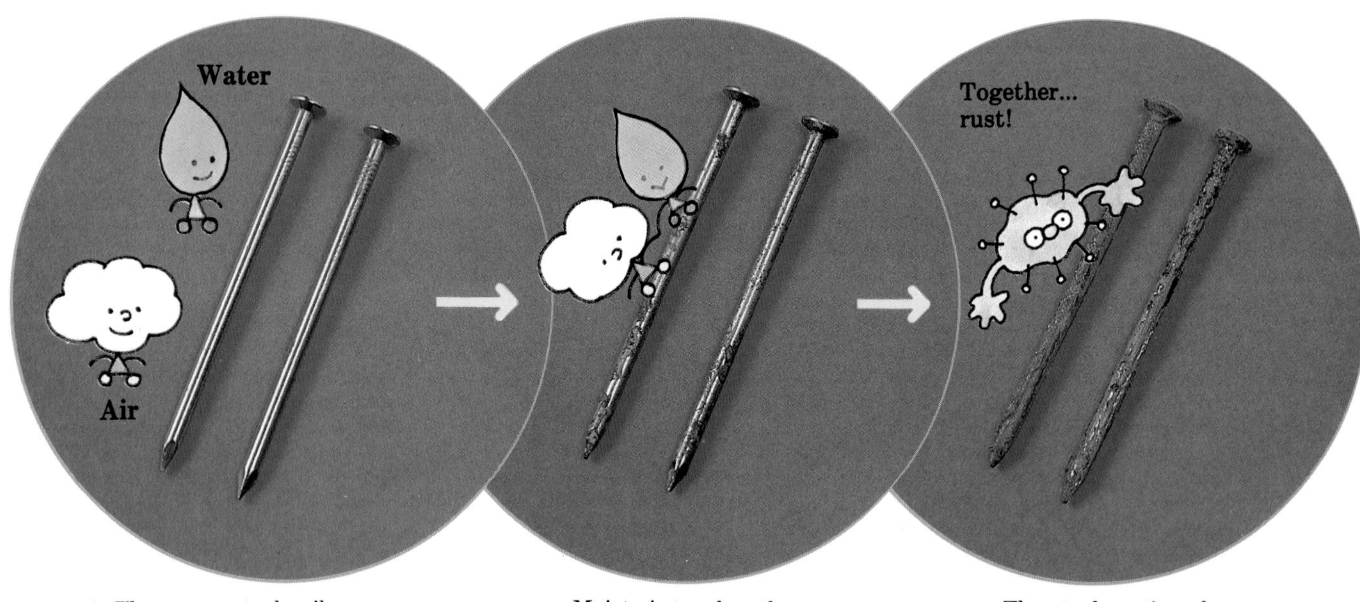

▲ These new steel nails are clean and shiny.

▲ Moist air touches them and they lose that shine.

▲ The steel coating changes into a rusty red color.

How Can We Stop Steel From Rusting?

To keep steel from rusting, we have to make sure water and air can't reach it. We can do that by painting the steel or by rubbing it with grease or oil. Or we can put on a thin coat of some metal that won't rust. That's called plating.

Painting

Coating with oil

Plating. Your bike handlebars are made of steel. But the shiny surface is really a thin coat of chrome, another metal, which protects the steel from rust.

Steel that doesn't rust easily

We mix metals that don't rust with steel to make stainless steel. It doesn't rust quickly.

These table things are stainless steel.

Some kitchen utensils are made of steel.

This entire sink is stainless steel.

• To the Parent

Rust is the result of a chemical reaction (oxidation) between steel and oxygen. Water speeds the process. Oxygen from the air dissolves in moisture on the surface of the steel, then rust starts to form. Once it starts, it continues. Untreated steel surfaces must be kept absolutely dry to prevent rust. Stainless steel resists rust because two other metals, chrome and nickel, are alloyed in it. These do not rust. That is why so many kitchen utensils are made from stainless steel.

Why Do Magnets Attract Steel?

ANSWER A magnet is made of iron or steel. Its tiniest bits, called atoms, pull together. If steel is near, it pulls on its atoms, and the steel sticks.

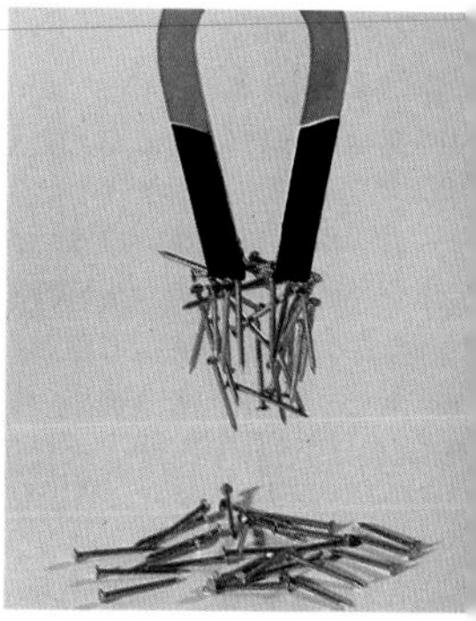

Magnets pick up only things made of iron or steel.

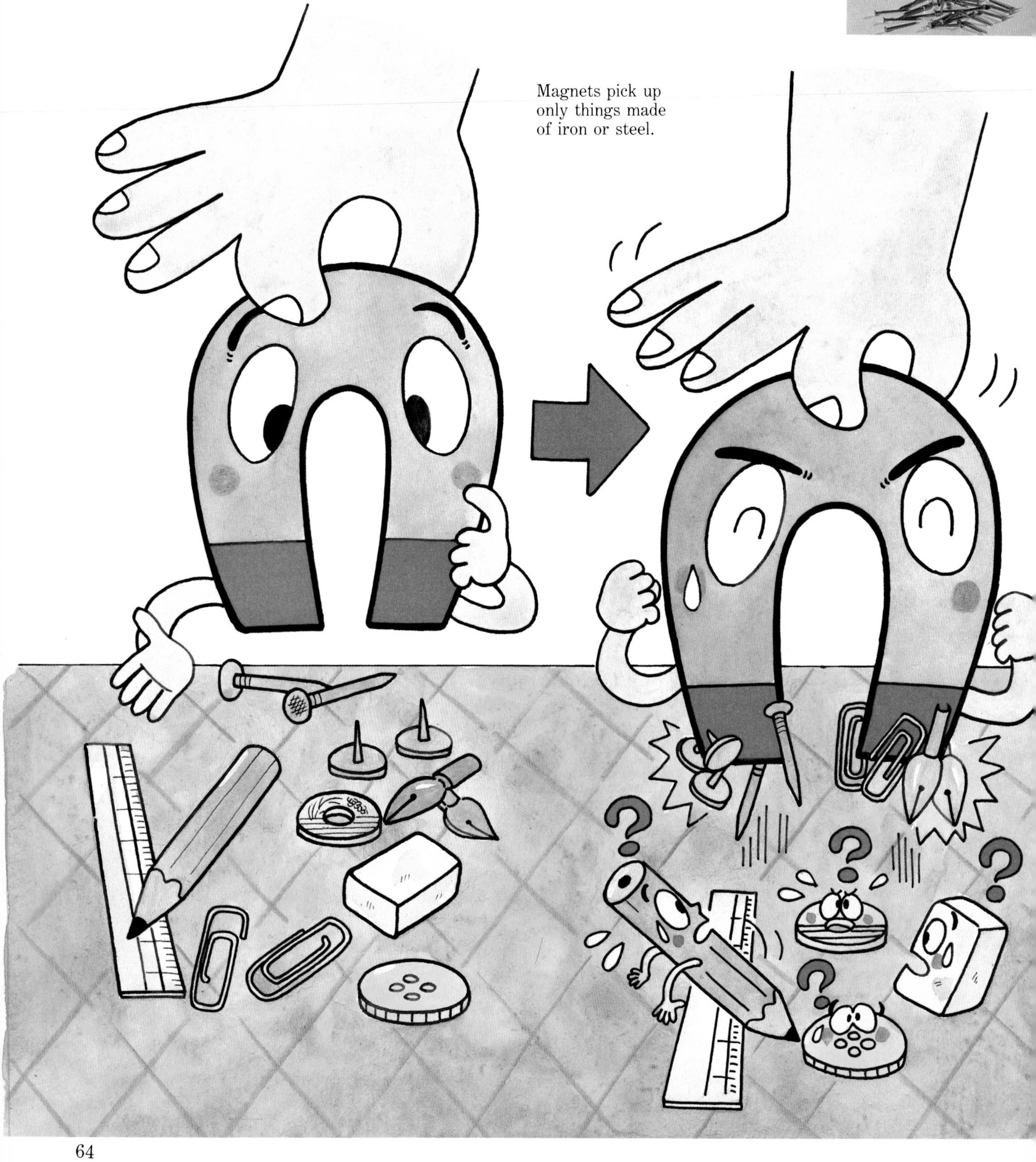

Steel touching a magnet acts magnetic too, so it sticks.

We've got to stick together!
We are!
I've got atomic power now. Stick with me!
Hey, I'm stuck. I mean I'm not stuck! H-e-l-p!

• To the Parent

The atoms in common steel are oriented in a random fashion. But in a permanent magnet they are all pointed in the same direction, so their magnetic properties come into play. That is why a magnet broken in half yields not one piece with a south pole and one with a north, but two that possess both poles. When ordinary steel or iron contacts a magnet, its atoms temporarily reorient in a single direction, so that the magnetism is transmitted. Nickel and cobalt act the same way.

The Many Uses of Magnets

Magnets are used in many of your toys. But they also make important things that we use every day. Can you think of some?

▲ **Magnets hold memos**

▶ **Magnets make toys move**

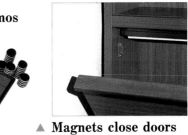

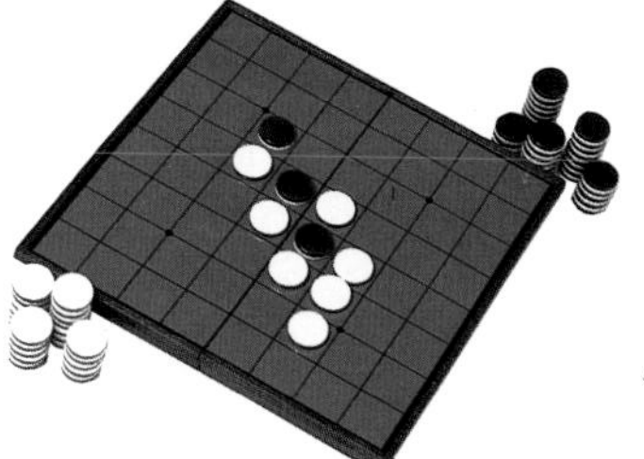

▲ **Magnets in board games**

▲ **Magnets close doors**

▲ **They can stick a marker on a car**

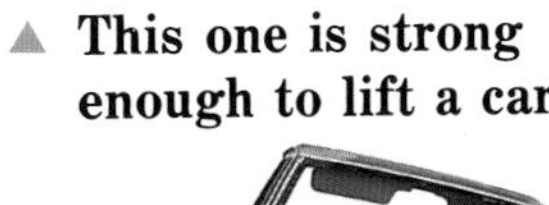

▲ **This one is strong enough to lift a car**

How Does a Magnifying Glass Work?

ANSWER A magnifying glass is thicker in the center. The thicker glass bends light before it reaches your eye, making things under the glass look bigger.

Why things look so much bigger

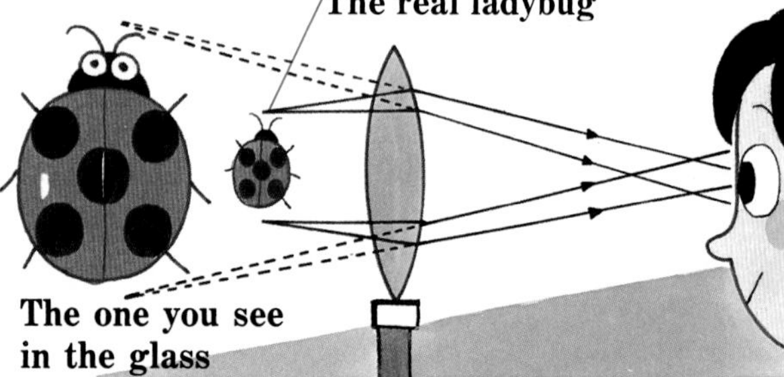

▲ The light rays it gives off are widened, then focused on your eye.

• To the Parent

A lens is either convex (thicker in the middle), or concave (thinner). Convex lenses magnify, and in spectacles they correct farsightedness. In mirror form they also magnify light beams from lighthouses. Convex lenses make things that are close appear to be larger but distant objects smaller and upside-down. Concave lenses correct nearsighted vision conditions by focusing light rays to a larger area. Convex lenses like the one shown above focus them to a smaller area.

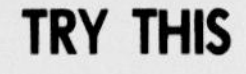

TRY THIS

Turn things upside down

Hold the magnifying glass out. Now things far away are smaller — and upside down.

TRY THIS

Look through nature's own lenses

Anything that we can see through, and that is thicker in the middle, makes things look bigger.

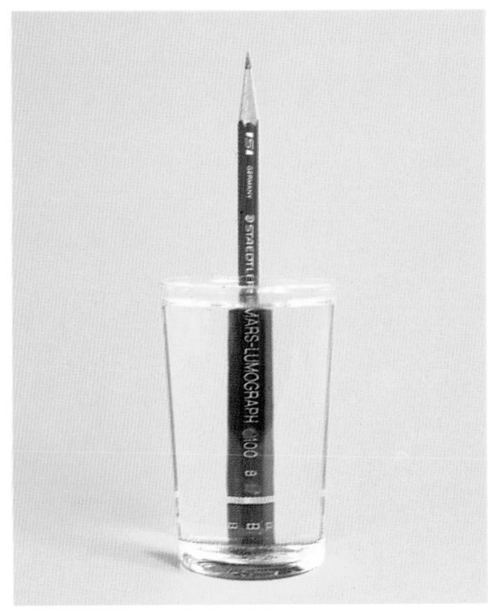

▲ **Water in a glass**

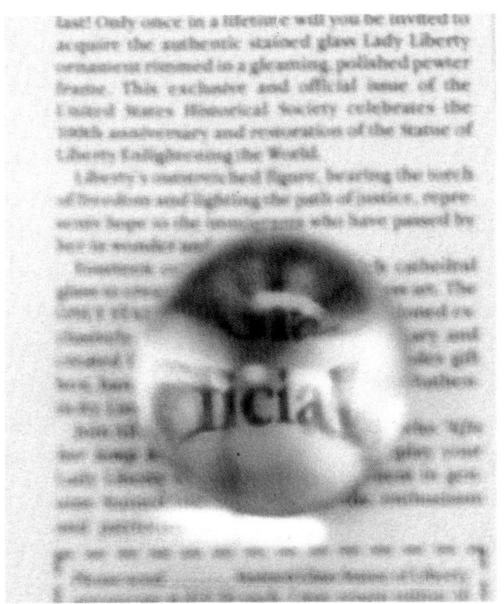

▲ **Glass marble.** If it is clear, a plain marble will make print appear larger, though it won't show much of the print.

Microscopes and telescopes

Both of these are to make things look bigger. Both do it with lenses.

▲ **Microscopes**
They let us look at things too small to be seen with our eyes alone.

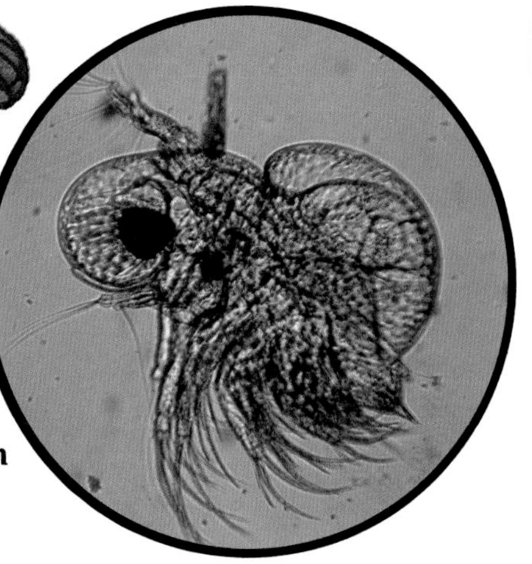

▶ **Water flea through a microscope**

▲ **Telescopes**
They make things far away seem near to us.

Why Does Soap Make Bubbles?

ANSWER Because the soap forms a film that traps air when you blow into it. If you are very careful not to blow too hard, the bubble will get very big without bursting.

Bubbles form when you blow air into the soap film

▶ The sticky film seals itself in a ball to hold the air inside.

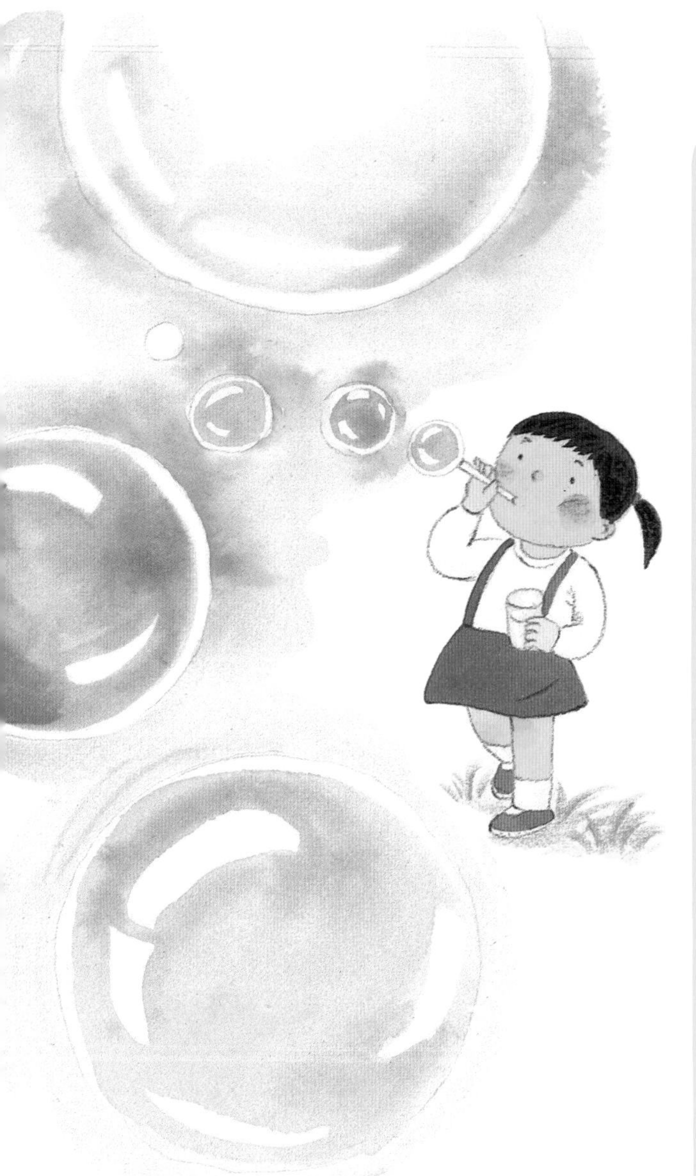

TRY THIS

A rainbow bubble

When you blow a soap bubble in the sunlight you can see a beautiful rainbow shining on the side.

◀ If the bubble is small it's hard to see.

▼ But when it's big just look at the colors!

TRY THIS

You can blow lots of bubbles all at once

▲ Twisted wire

▼ on a straw is all you need.

Twist lots of loops into the wire, and slip it into the end of the straw. Dip it in soap and blow!

• To the Parent

Soap and water will form a thin but very strong film. When air is blown into this film it raises a bubble. When the bubble separates from the rest of the film it seals itself through its own surface tension. That tension is what makes the bubble a perfect globe and gives it its great strength. As the bubble grows the film gets thinner and thinner. Rays of sunlight are separated as if by a prism, and that is what makes the rainbow.

How Does Glue Work?

ANSWER 1 Wood and paper have tiny holes on their surface. Glue gets into them, dries and holds things together.

ANSWER 2 When some glue mixes, chemical changes take place. Superstrong glue becomes a part of the pieces it touches. Glue is used even in the concrete blocks that make up elevated highways. Different kinds of glue are used in many car parts and airplane parts too.

Different Kinds of Glue

There are many kinds of glue. Some are made from natural things like bones and the skin of animals. Others are made from chemicals that are strong in water.

Regular glue is made from the skin and bones of animals. It's very strong, but it can come apart in water.

Mucilage is made from water and plants. It's not strong, but it's good for gluing pieces of paper together.

Paste is made by mixing flour and water. It's easy to make even at home, and it's very good on all kinds of paper.

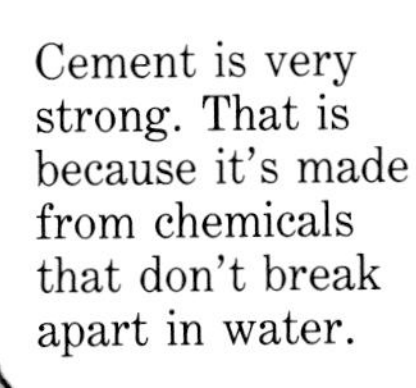

Cement is very strong. That is because it's made from chemicals that don't break apart in water.

• To the Parent

True glue is made from the skin and bones of animals, although the term is now commonly used for a variety of adhesive products. Among the different kinds of glue available the most common are the paste, mucilage and cement used to repair household products and appliances. Glue bonds in several ways. In mechanical bonding the glue fills in surface pores and physically holds two surfaces together. In chemical bonding the adhesive unites chemically with the surface of the pieces being joined, and some glues bond at the molecular level creating magnetic-like attractions between items. Adhesion can be strong or weak, depending on the kind of bonding.

What Happens to Letters That We Mail?

ANSWER Post office workers collect them to be sent to the people we write to.

▼ **The mail carrier takes the letters from the mail box to the post office and other mail carriers deliver them.**

MINI-DATA

Some of the world's mail boxes

It would be a lot of trouble if we had to go to the post office each time we wanted to send off a letter, so there are boxes on the streets to put letters into. The boxes at right are used by three European countries.

▲ Sweden's mail box

▲ **A red one in Holland**

▲ **What the French use**

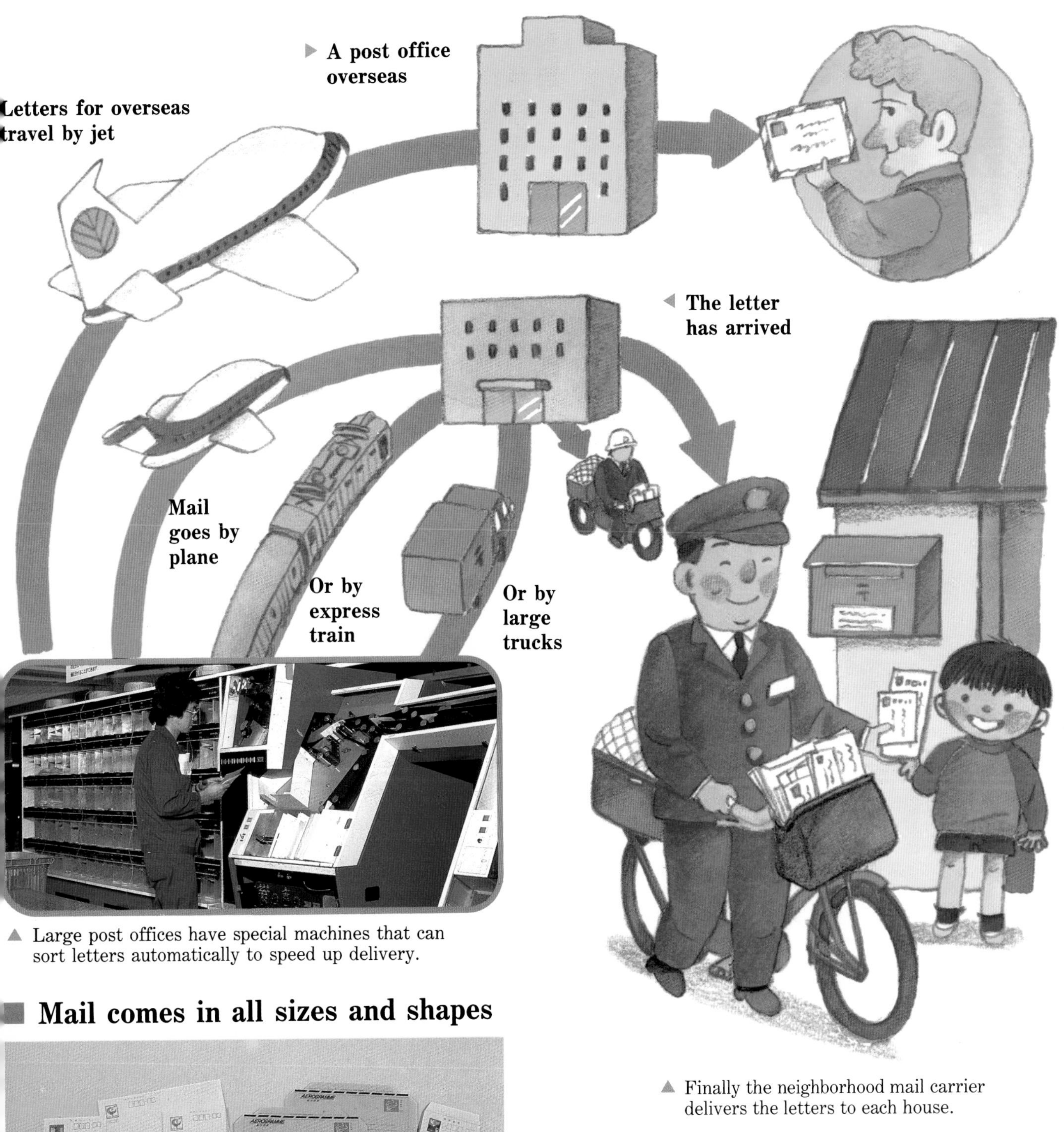
A post office overseas
Letters for overseas travel by jet
The letter has arrived
Mail goes by plane
Or by express train
Or by large trucks

▲ Large post offices have special machines that can sort letters automatically to speed up delivery.

▲ Finally the neighborhood mail carrier delivers the letters to each house.

Mail comes in all sizes and shapes

▲ Letters and cards from different countries

• To the Parent

Much modernization, such as big automated sorting machines for high-speed handling, has affected the postal service in central cities. And of course big jets now speed airmail letters to any point on the globe within days. Nevertheless most of us think of postal service as just the handy mail box or the letter slot, or faithful mail carriers on their daily rounds. Most countries use numerical codes for addresses to make it easier to sort mail and increase speed of delivery.

How Does a Vending Machine Work?

Inside the machine are large racks of the things you want. The machine counts your coins, and when you press a button it drops one of its items into a slot at the bottom.

Here's a canned drink type of machine. See the cans? The machine is cold inside like a refrigerator.

The cold cans come out at this slot, one at a time, after you've put in the right amount of money.

The pocket in the door lets you reach into the slot and take out the thing you have bought.

Down here is where the refrigerator machinery is. It makes sure each drink is cold when you buy it.

A Few Vending Machines

There are vending machines for almost everything. You can buy newspapers, cold drinks, ice cream, laundry soap at the laundromat, magazines, even clothing from these machines. They are in many neighborhoods and so are convenient for purchase of small items that we don't want to make a trip to the store for.

◀ A newspaper vendor

Some nice French snacks ▶

our favorite soft drinks ▶

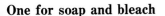

One for soap and bleach

▼ Ticket vending machine

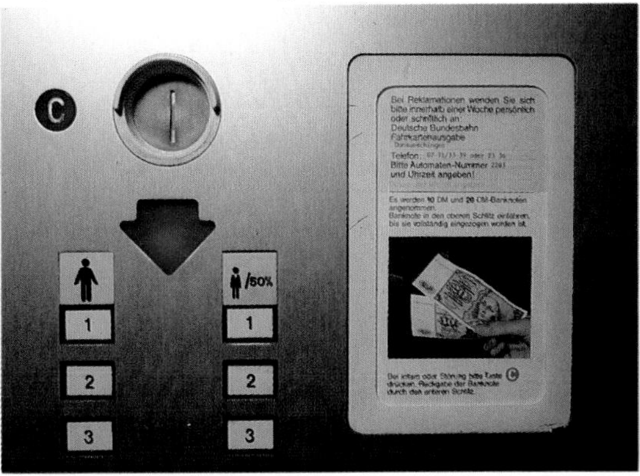

● **To the Parent**

Vending machines have become more familiar to us with each passing day and now are an important sector of the retail industry. They allow around-the-clock sales, they can be located conveniently close to the customer and what's more they reduce the labor costs of the retailer. Customers need not wait to make their purchases. Yet a growing problem in the case of beverages and foods has been the proper disposal of empty containers. Please remind everyone not to litter!

Why Can't a Car Stop Quickly?

ANSWER A moving car is pushing its weight forward. It's very heavy, so the faster it goes, the harder it is to stop.

TRY THIS

Run, then stop quickly

When you're walking it's easy to stop at once. But when you run it's harder.

The Faster a Car Goes, the Longer It Takes to Stop

A car moving slowly can stop quickly. One moving faster takes more time to slow down.

If it's going very slowly, about 12 miles (20 km) an hour, it can stop in only about 30 feet (9 m).

A car moving at a speed of 25 miles (40 km) an hour takes 75 feet (23 m) to come to a halt.

A car traveling 60 miles (100 km) an hour will run about 325 feet (100 m) before it comes to a stop.

Always use your bicycle brakes safety!

A speeding bicycle also will take a longer time to stop.

Be alert and brake early.

▸ If you have front and back brakes use the back ones first. If you don't, you could flip over!

• To the Parent

The basic laws of motion declare that all moving bodies tend to continue moving but that those at rest will continue to remain at rest. And the greater the speed, the greater is the effect of this principle. Moreover, a motor vehicle's stopping distance is very greatly influenced by weight of the vehicle and the load, and by surface conditions as well as by the driver's reaction time. A child's safety depends on whether he or she understands this.

What Do We Have Here?

Tea bushes

Tea is made of the leaves of tea bushes. They are picked when they're new each spring, then steamed and dried. We put them in hot water to make tea.

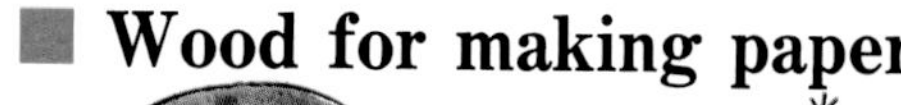

Wood for making paper

This is a big pile of small chips of wood. They are soaked in chemicals, mashed into a kind of soup, then squeezed into thin sheets on a roller.

Raw plastic before it is made into shapes

To make toys and other things from it, plastic is heated until it's soft. The softened plastic is then carefully poured into molds of toy shapes and allowed to cool.

Inside a music box

When you wind up the spring (1) the drum (2) begins to turn. The tiny bumps covering the drum each pluck a metal strip (3), and each makes a note!

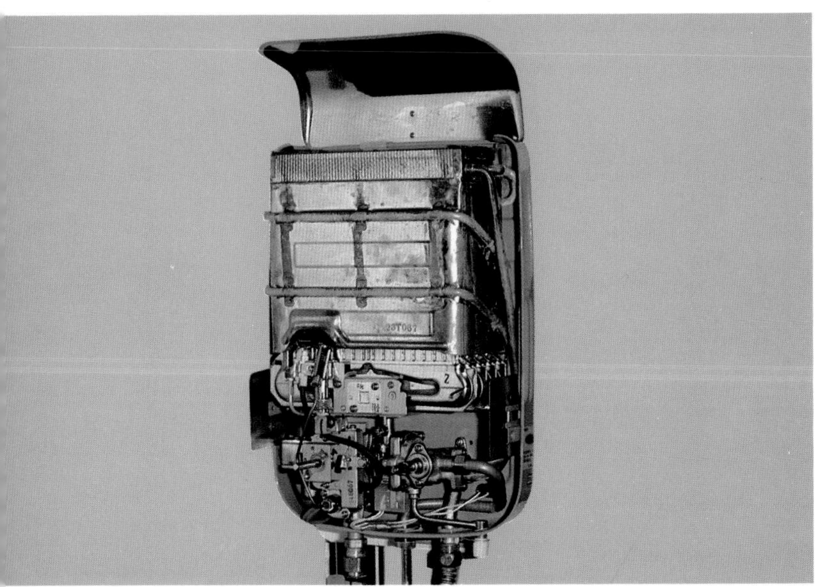

Inside a water heater

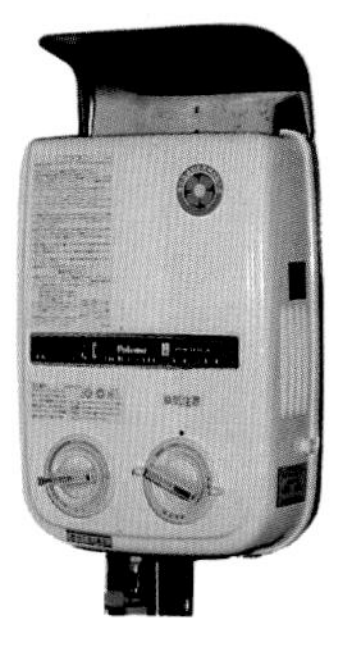

See the long, twisting tube? Water flows through it while gas flames shoot up from below. The water is heated from the outside as it moves along.

Inside an electronic game

You can't see the electricity, but you can see the screen with the figures that move. It's the square part.

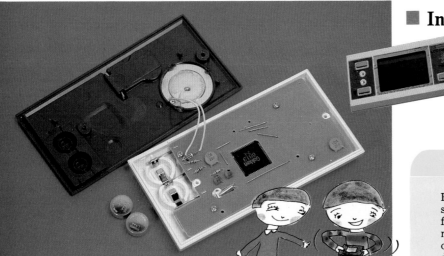

• To the Parent

Black and green teas both grow on the same kind of plant, but black tea is fermented in processing. Opening up a music box is usually easy to do. But opening a water heater is extremely dangerous, and opening an electronic game case can destroy the entire game.

Do You Know What These Things Are?

Fire hydrant

Its shape is different from most hydrants that you see, but it carries water for fighting fires just like the rest of them.

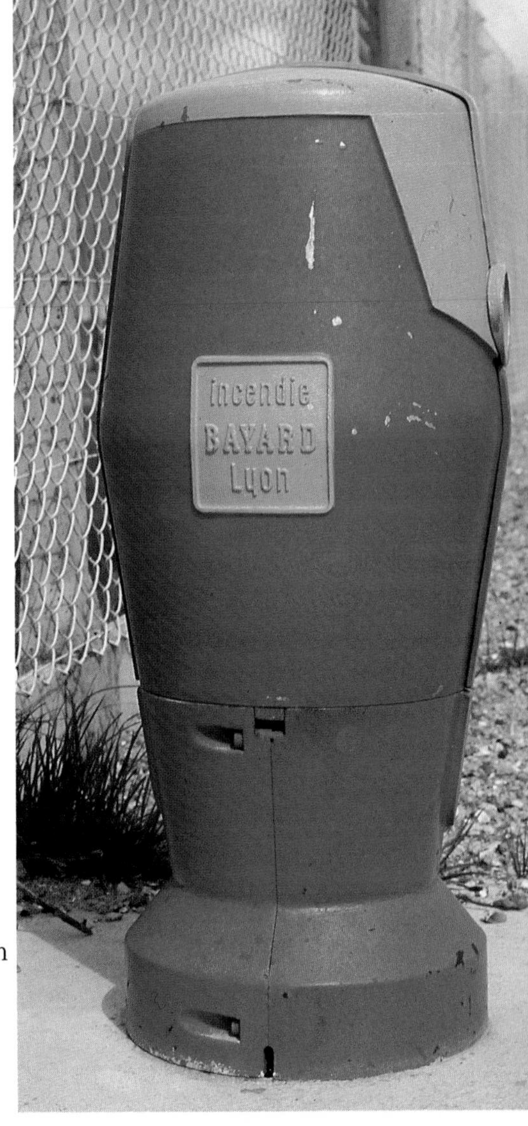

Electric cable

Wires like this are used for telephones, TV and other things. The colors help the workers if the wires need some repairs.

Lighthouse

It's an unusual angle so you might not recognize it. Its light keeps ships from running aground on rocks off the coastline.

• To the Parent

Colored wires are vital in applications like jet planes, where a mistake on a wire could mean disaster. Lighthouses get their names from their lights, and manholes are so named since repair people often crawl through them.

Manhole cover

Many streets have pipes, sewers and cables under them. Workers go through manholes when they must make re

Growing-Up Album

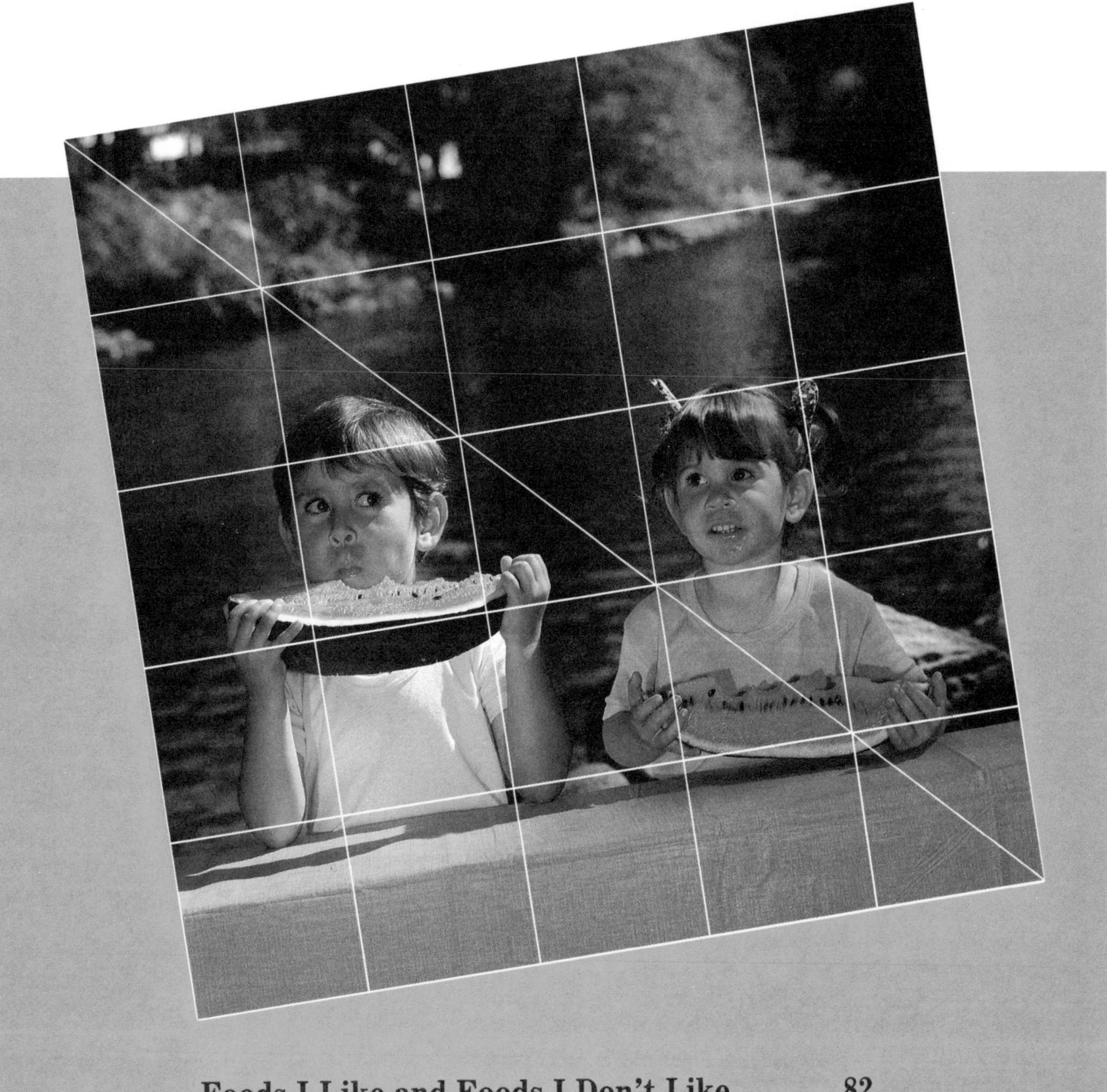

Foods I Like and Foods I Don't Like.......82
The Toys I Like to Play With Most........84
People and Things I See...................85
Here Are Some Riddles....................86

Foods I Like and Foods I Don't Like

Probably no subject in child-raising causes more controversy, and sometimes trouble, than the foods children want or refuse to eat. It is said that these preferences are learned from parents, but that is an unproven assumption. And it is certain in any case that likes and dislikes can easily change over the years. It might be instructive to record what your child eats and then ask your doctor how well the nutritional content meets his or her growth needs.

■ Mark the things you like with an O and the things you don't like with an X

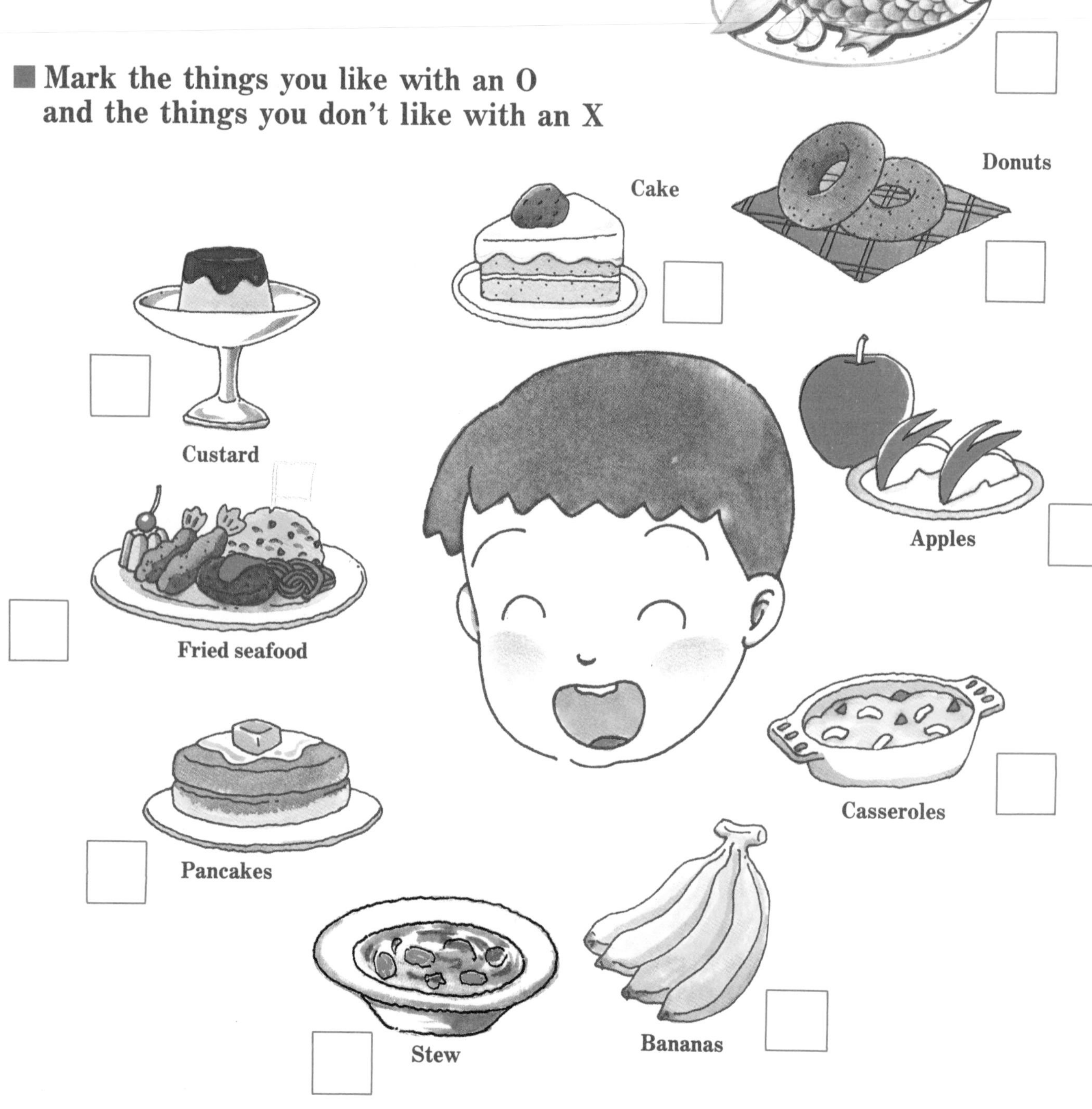

These are my favorite foods:

These are foods I don't like:

The Toys I Like to Play With Most

People and Things I See

Goldfish

My Grandfather and Grandmother

Cats

Food

My shoes

Dolls

Milk

Cars

Other things I see:

People I see:

Here Are Some Riddles

■ **The answers are all in the picture. Can you find them?**

1. What has one long hand and one short hand, and moves all day?
2. What talks and shows pictures but never moves?
3. What has four strong legs but doesn't move them?
4. What do you open when you go out but never when you go in?
5. What must always take off its cap before it can go to work?
6. Where in your house is it always cold?
7. What does water go into and steam come out of?
8. What gets smaller as you get bigger?

1. A clock 2. A television 3. A chair 4. An umbrella
5. A fountain pen 6. In the refrigerator 7. A kettle
8. Your clothes

A Child's First Library of Learning

Things Around Us

Time-Life Books is a division of
Time Life Inc., a wholly owned
subsidiary of The Time Inc. Book Company
Time-Life Books, Alexandria, Virginia
Children's Publishing

Director: Robert H. Smith
Associate Director: R. S. Wotkyns III
Editorial Director: Neil Kagan
Promotion Director: Kathleen Tresnak
Editorial Consultants: Jacqueline A. Ball, Andrew Gutelle

Editorial Supervision by:
International Editorial Services, Inc.
Tokyo, Japan

Editor: C. E. Berry
Editorial Research: Miki Ishii
Design: Kim Bolitho
Writer: Pauline Bush
Educational Consultants: Janette Bryden, Laurie Hanawa
Translation: Ronald K. Jones

TIME LIFE®

Library of Congress Cataloging in Publication Data
Things around us.
p. cm. — (A Child's first library of learning)
Summary: Questions and answers present some of life's everyday mysteries, such as why steel rusts, why soap gets things clean, and how plants grow.
ISBN 0-8094-4845-9. ISBN 0-8094-4846-7 (lib. bdg.)
1. Science—Miscellanea—Juvenile literature.
[1. Science—Miscellanea. 2. Questions and answers.] I. Time-Life Books. II. Series.
Q163.T48 1989 500—dc19 88-36632

Fifth printing 1993. Printed in U.S.A.
Published simultaneously in Canada.